Hilary McPhee founded McPhee Gribble Publishers with Diana Gribble in 1975. After Penguin Books Australia acquired the company's assets at the end of 1989 she remained with the imprint as publisher for two years before joining Pan Macmillan. From 1994 to 1997 she was Chair of the Australia Council and of the Major Organizations Board and is at present Vice Chancellor's Fellow at the University of Melbourne.

Hilary McPhee

Other People's
WORDS

PICADOR
Pan Macmillan Australia

First published 2001 in Picador by Pan Macmillan Australia Pty Limited
This edition published 2002 in Picador by Pan Macmillan Australia Pty Limited
St Martins Tower, 31 Market Street, Sydney

National Library of Australia
Cataloguing-in-Publication data:

McPhee, Hilary, 1941– .
Other people's words.

ISBN 0 330 36342 5 (pbk).

1. McPhee, Hilary, 1941– . 2. Gribble, Diana, 1942– .
3. McPhee Gribble Publishers. 4. Publishers and publishing – Australia.
5. Authors, Australian – 20th century. I. Title.

070.50994

Typeset in Bembo Roman by Post Pre-press Group
Printed in Australia by McPherson's Printing Group

Cover and text design by Gayna Murphy, Greendot Design

FOR HARRIET AND RUPERT FREEMAN,
FREYA, MATTHEW AND JAMES MICHIE, ELLIE WATSON
AND MY GOD-DAUGHTER ANNA GRIBBLE

Contents

Part One

The other world – the old world, the land hemisphere – is far above her as it is shown on maps drawn upside-down by old world cartographers. From that world and particularly from a scarcely noticeable island up toward the North Pole the people came, all by steam; or their parents, all by sail. And there they live round the many thousand miles of seaboard, hugging the water and the coastal rim. Inside, over the Blue Mountains, are the plains heavy with wheat, then the endless dust, and after outcrops of silver, opal, and gold, Sahara, the salt-encrusted bed of a prehistoric sea, and leafless mountain ranges. There is nothing in the interior; so people look to the water, and above to the fixed stars and constellations which first guided men there.

Christina Stead, *For Love Alone*,
Peter Davies, 1945, p.1

1

First Words

First came her stories like webs across the world. They crisscrossed the Atlantic on steamers and the Rockies by train. They made their way down dirt tracks where the scrub met overhead. They flew from Ben Lomond in the Tasmanian Highlands, which we could see from her verandah, to Welsh farmhouses of dark stone. The air would shiver slightly each time she began.

Once upon a time, when pigs were swine and monkeys chewed tobacco, there was a little girl who lived at the foot of the mountains in the centre of the universe at the bottom of the world . . .

The story-teller was my grandmother and the child was me. We came to her for stories. She had a way of making herself ready, hands folded in her lap, cushions at her back. Her stories were vivid and shapely and we heard them again and again. In the night under the pine trees, her house creaked and her stories invaded our dreams. Later I would catch something of their rhythms and word play in ballads and sagas and know what a talented story-teller she was. Then we took her for granted.

These days I tell her stories to my extended family, but they must compete with sound bytes and flashbacks, videoclips and computer games. And I have no doubt I fail to tell them as well as she did for I have the rapt attention of small children only in short bursts. My grandmother could keep us by her side for hours.

An early memory is of her in a cane chair in the garden. There is a heat wave and she is trading her stories for buckets of water.

Only when she is soaked to the skin will she begin. *Once upon a time . . .* On the farm, travelling in the back of the ute with the children, she swathed in scarves in an old armchair and we under quilts, trembling with fear as she spins tales of murder and mayhem in the dark houses glimpsed from the road. But best of all were the stories at the end of the day when I'd creep into her bed, the lamp turned low. Then my soft and powdery grandmother, her black hair in a long plait, would start. *Once upon a time, when pigs were swine . . .*

She was born in 1894, a beloved only child in a family with a little money or the myth of money from her great-great-grandfather, a clergyman, who had invested during the early nineteenth century, surely somewhat dubiously, in Welsh coalmines. Family portraits survive and hang in a Tasmanian dining-room.

I know I should check the facts. There is evidence

to be weighed, archives to be searched, family members still alive who knew her differently. There will be shipping lists and parish records, deeds and wills lodged in three countries. The men I will find easily, labelled by their work and their bank balances, the buying and selling of land, and of houses returned to at night. The women will have left less clear a mark on the record but more of a mark on me, perhaps, and on all the children in between. There are some family papers, recipes, photographs and a sampler in black cross-stitch done, my grandmother told me, by a child, my great-great-great-great-grandmother, during the Napoleonic wars when children were forbidden to use coloured silks. Or so she said.

There were stories of unfeeling trustees and money withheld and unsuitable marriages when good-looking rogues took advantage of well-to-do widows – one of whom was my great-grandmother. She seems to have married an American twenty years her junior after my great-grandfather died. This young man went into the city of London every morning at ten *but never told his wife what he did there*. Perhaps she never asked. When it was discovered that he'd been through all her money, he returned to America, never to be seen again. Or so the story goes.

After my grandmother died, I found in her bedroom photographs of a picnic by a lake, taken about 1910. And there is the American husband, her step-father, dangerously handsome and very young, in expensive-looking tweeds and brogues. My great-grandmother, his wife, is dumpy and distinctly middle-aged. She looks cross and unhappy, not at all the dashing figure of my imaginings. He is propped up on an elbow smiling calmly at the camera. Maybe for him it was all worth it – or maybe he has been maligned. Perhaps, somewhere in America, other pieces of the story I have not heard were planted in the heads of American children – cookies and lemonade to hand – stories where my great-grandmother has become a wicked old English witch who made a fine young man's life a misery.

The historian at the back of my brain says I should discover what is true and what is false, make a properly considered account before it's too late. The rest of me, the part that was shaped by the sense of myself *at the centre of the universe at the bottom of the world*, still sees, as if through certain cloud formations above paddocks pale with tussocks, the shapes and shadows of other places she made my own.

I want to leave her and her stories be.

I know the sound a cotton reel makes when it rattles against a wooden leg in a box under a bed. There was a great-great-great-great-great-grandmother who was born during the French Revolution, a very old woman indeed by the time my grandmother's mother as a little girl was taken to visit her. She saw her wrinkled face and corkscrew curls against lacy pillows – for she was a vain old woman – and was shown, as a special treat, the wooden leg. I know the lavender and starched smells of the linen closet where the children hid and pulled on the thread, making the reel rattle in the box and the old lady call for her maid: 'Bless me, Lizzie, there's a mouse in my leg.'

The historian counts down the generations to see if this is possible – but I was there, whatever the facts of the matter. I smelt coal dust from the coalhole beneath the pavement in a London street, heard the cry of the cats' meat man as he tossed lumps of offal every morning over the iron railings, tasted roast chestnuts bought from braziers in the snow on the way to church, heard the shouts of guards and the heavy sounds of doors slamming on steam trains leaving country stations.

I have her autograph book full of poems and drawings and jokes in French, German and Italian, from 1907-8 which she spent in a Swiss finishing school learning European pronunciations, for she wanted very much to be a singer. There is the handwriting of the two elderly *M'selles* who owned the school and wore the same black dresses every day and smelt of old hay. I recognize Muriel Mamby, Katerina Gründlich, Aline Collière from her stories and know how they hoisted themselves over the school wall to eat hot bread rolls filled with chocolate from the baker. And soon grew too fat for their corsets.

Then came the stories of endless wheatfields and sleeping for a week on the train to Vancouver. And catching the very last ship to Sydney before war was declared. The one-room school at Kettering in southern Tasmania where the children from England went barefoot like the others, hiding their new shoes in the bushes. Picnics on Bruny Island and Guy Fawkes Night in Syd's paddock with raspberry cordial and sausages grilled on burning stumps in the dark. And Hector the dog riding on the running board of the old Dodge car, into long summers under canvas and rockpools full of lobsters. Until the stories arrive at the romance at the centre of my universe.

It had all begun, my grandmother said, on a cold winter's night on a railway station in Gippsland. I picture them in black and white like the films of the day. It is night and a young man, rain pouring off his hat, waits for the train from Melbourne. He is, of course, tall, dark and very handsome and the young woman travelling towards him will fall in love with him on the spot, or so the story has it. I picture the pale faces of the man and the woman searching for each other so they can begin their lives together and become my parents.

Where the young man, my father, came from was not part of the story. He arrived mysteriously, fully formed, as it were, and stepped into the part that was awaiting him.

His family story amounted to less than a paragraph, the kind you could find in any Scottish guide book. The departure in small boats from Colonsay to Skye in the seventeenth century, the clearing of the glens to make way for sheep, a famine and a family shipped to Australia to start again. All that history – and only one glimpse survived that he gave me late in his life. A white-bearded old man at the head of the table in the kitchen of a farmhouse somewhere in the countryside, is speaking in Gaelic. On either side of him are ranged many children and their parents.

My father as a boy was given this image, for it does not have a story's shape, by his father. Where the farm was we did not know, nor who it was at the head of the table. My father did not tell us and we did not think to ask. He was not a story-teller, my father, content, it seemed, to be a player in the tales of women.

Not until much later did it occur to me to search the records for the old man who spoke Gaelic at table, in the only account I have from that side of the family. And there he was, easily found – as a young boy from the glens of Sligachan at the foot of the Cuillin Hills on Skye, shipped with his parents and twenty-seven members of his family to Port Phillip in 1853. And there, too, was his marriage in 1869 to the granddaughter of Martha, who kept the inn at Faithfulls Creek.

The day we find the grave it is early spring. River gums and stringy barks line the track beside the creek by the Strathbogie Ranges in north-eastern Victoria not far from the highway I have travelled many times on the way to somewhere else. In this beautiful place the silence at first is absolute.

The grave on the bank of Faithfulls Creek belongs to Martha who arrived in Australia from Scotland in 1837, the wife of an overseer near Goulburn in New South Wales. A few years later, they were the owners of the Stockman's Rest, a slab hut beside the creek, an inn for shepherds and stockmen travelling the stock route south towards Port Phillip. In summer the heat in the broad valley would be fierce and in winter the creek must have flooded the track.

Martha died in childbirth in 1848, and her last baby was suckled on a goat. Or so the story, repeated in newspaper accounts each time a 'pioneer of the district' died, would have it. What is not mentioned is that the creek is named for the Faithfull brothers, William Pitt and George, forever linked to the killings – the Faithfull Massacre – that took place not far from here at the Winding Swamp on the Broken River in April 1838.

William Pitt Faithfull, the elder son of a soldier in the Rum Corps, had set out from Goulburn to secure for himself some of the rich pastures south of the Murray. A large convoy of eighteen shepherds, assigned convicts and ticket-of-leavers most of them, 3472 sheep and 395 cattle were sent ahead. By 6 April 1838 they were camped at the Winding Swamp.

The accounts that were sent north in the next few weeks describe an attack by as many as three hundred and as few as twenty Pangerang warriors, in which eight of the shepherds were killed and stock scattered. Faithfull's retaliations went on for many weeks. Large numbers of Pangerang men, women and children were killed and their bodies 'burnt on the spot to hide their unlawful act'.

Faithfull's massacre has come to describe both the

largest number of whites slain in a single attack in
the colony's history and the reprisals which were
among the worst; events that thwarted Governor
Gipps' declaration to the colony that Aborigines
were to be 'accorded special "protection" from
European aggression', and 'henceforth regarded as
equal subjects of the Queen, treated with loving
"sympathy and kindness"'.

Few Aborigines were seen again around the
Strathbogie pastoral runs. Silence is said to have
descended. The story became 'Benalla's secret', wrote
a schoolteacher in 1900.[1]

The silence is an official silence – of local records,
municipal offices and friendly museums full of family
bric-à-brac, farmers' tools and photographs. In a
close knit district the histories written are careful. By
the turn of the century families on small selections
alongside brothers and cousins have planted fruit trees
beside the creek, split their logs and fenced their
blocks. The school rolls list children from half a
dozen large families who shared the past – but were
no doubt more conscious of their late Victorian,
newly federated, drought-afflicted, present.

Were questions never asked or stories told?

The real stories in my family, the ones that sound too
good to be true, even to me, with patterns and
rhythms I never forgot – the real stories stretched

back and forth through my mother's family. My mother and my grandmother exchanged letters every week across Bass Strait, their remarkably similar round and rapid handwriting weaving the drama of everyday life, and, when suitable bits were read out at mealtimes, holding us all.

And then there were the books. My grandmother's little house was full of them. Bookshelves lined the main room with its bread oven in the hearth, and covered the top of the upright piano. Her bedroom was a mess: clothes on chairs, books everywhere. She had a standing order with the State Library which sent books to her each month in a wooden crate, and with Robertson & Mullens in Elizabeth Street, Melbourne, who knew her tastes, for new books on approval. There would be parcels to be collected at the post office counter in the general store or at the railway siding whenever I stayed with her. We would lie on our beds after lunch, a tin of Marie biscuits on the chest of drawers between us, and read until dark.

It was inconceivable to be without a book. No train was boarded without buying something to read for the journey – the new Puffins for us, an *Argosy*, a *Lilliput* or a Penguin paperback for her.

Allen Lane, the founder of Penguin Books in England, was one of my grandmother's heroes. Her heroes were many and diverse and, naturally, all men. They ranged from George VI, for a time Major Douglas of Douglas Social Credit, to Bertrand Russell, the Beatles – and Allen Lane.

Penguin Books, which Lane had established in

1935, to publish for 'the intelligent layman', was a product of a philosophy which had emerged in Britain in the 1930s through the BBC, the Workers' Educational Association and the Left Book Club. By providing serious subjects and quality fiction in mass-produced paperback formats 'for the price of a packet of cigarettes' (6d), Lane created a revolution that must be one of the most democratic success stories in twentieth-century social history.

Penguin Books rapidly embedded itself in the reading habits of Australians – and of people like my grandmother, who would never have regarded herself as anything other than an Englishwoman who happened to find herself living abroad. The democratic revolution would not have meant a great deal to her – but to have inexpensive international writing at railway station bookstalls, in country newsagents and bookshops in Hobart and Launceston was her link to a larger world.

She had every Penguin from No. 1 – thrillers, novels, Pelicans – until they changed the covers in the mid-1960s, when she wrote sternly to Allen Lane about the paperbacks looking too American, the dangers of dumbing-down – or whatever was then the equivalent.

Her reading was as real to her as life was. She would talk about the characters in a book and people she met, eccentric at best, certifiable at worst, the tragic farewell she'd watched at the bus stop, with the same intensity and curiosity. Dickens, Trollope, George Eliot, W.H. Ainsworth, Thackeray, Buchan,

Shaw: they were prisms and she described her own life refracted through theirs. Her England, to which she never returned or even seemed to long for, was kept alive forever in those stories and nineteenth-century novels.

Later, when she began long treks to the first film festivals, she'd return with the stories in her head as if she'd been inside the film. I first heard the story of *The Wages of Fear* in her little house with the wind howling through the pine trees. So vividly did my grandmother describe the journey down the mountain somewhere in Central America in the truck full of nitro-glycerine that could explode at any moment that, when I saw the film years later, I recognized it scene by scene.

Not until I was in my twenties, having spent time in London and found myself to my surprise to be a passionate Australian fiercely critical of remnants of British imperialism and more attuned than I knew to the nuances of our provincial life, did I detect a note at times in her elderly voice of something very close to English condescension. I was dismayed, of course, and for a little while before she died, replayed self-righteously much of what she'd told me.

I didn't approve of the way she made funny stories in her long and sparkling weekly letters about the daily doings of the Tasmanian gentry and their rural labourers. Tasmania's convict history was of interest to her only in the lengths the locals went to deny it. The street of convict cottages that ran down to the river behind her house on my uncle's farm was simply there outside the window. But the mummified cat she'd found in one of the garrets sat on her mantelpiece for years with silver paper eyes – and crept, of course, into her stories. Yet she was the first person to tell me about the Black Line and the shell middens the children found on the beach at Oyster Cove long after the people who'd left them had been removed to Flinders Island. She made us turn away from Truganini's skeleton on permanent display in the Hobart Museum.

I heard her admiration of gentlemen English cricketers as anachronistic and grating. Despite a long life of great freedom and eccentricity, she behaved always as if men were centre stage, and there to be cajoled and flattered. She, the most independent of women, widowed at thirty-six, deeply disliked modern feminism. She wrote sternly on my second marriage in the mid-seventies that women could only be happy if they put men first.

Australian literature and theatre were irredeemably second rate for her. She attended local concerts and productions of plays in the absence of anything else but I cannot remember an Australian poem or novel she admired. This occurred to me at precisely the moment when I'd decided that they mattered to me a great deal.

Next to Arthur Mee's *Children's Encyclopedia* on the bookshelves in my parents' house was a brown leatherette-covered set of the *Modern World Ency-clopaedia*, published in England in 1935 by the Home Entertainment Library and given to my parents on their wedding day during the war. The entry on Australia describes the platypus and the echidna warmly. The Australian Government, we are told, has pursued 'an exclusive social policy' because 'the Aboriginal Race represents an archaic survival and are declining . . . their religion finds comfort in mythical cults, having as their base a confused worship of the forces of life.' There is no mention anywhere of a penal colony or of convicts. The origins of white settlement are hidden from sight. 'Australian Literature' begins with Charles Harpur and ends with *Robbery Under Arms* (1888).

I can shut my eyes and picture the books in their places on the cream-painted shelves. We knew they were the most important things in the house. I can conjure up the texture of their covers, the smell of their pages, their weight in my hands. Here were my father's school prizes, elaborately bound with marbled endpapers and tissue paper pages over each of the engravings, and a grim-looking volume of myths and legends without illustrations. My mother's university textbooks, her mother's Blackwell's pocketbook editions of Shakespeare's plays in ragged cloth covers and the prizes for civics and essay-writing won at the high school in the city when she went away to board.

In pride of place next to the encyclopedias and the Bible and covered in brown paper was F. Truby King's manual, *Baby and Childcare* of 1934, reprinted seven times to 1939. I somehow sensed, maybe because of the brown paper, that this was a text on which the household depended and I gazed at photographs of smiling blond children on verandahs somewhere in the Empire, the products, as I was, of fresh milk and regular sun baths even on the coldest days, children with clear eyes and straight legs, their proud mothers free of superstition and old wives' tales.

Truby King, authority on every aspect of child-care and mothering, including feelings which were better repressed, was born in New Zealand in 1858 and trained in Edinburgh. Paediatrician and eugeni-cist, he ruled innumerable households during the first half of the century. Truby King suited Empire – by catering for its insecurities. Second and third generation colonials in South Africa, Canada, Australia and New Zealand not yet sure of where they fitted in the world must have felt safer with his instructions and his strictures.

King's words were reassuring and sensible, some of them, especially in the days before household refrig-eration and when infant diarrhoea was a killer, or before penicillin when measles were dangerous and meningitis often fatal. Mothers living far from their families, as many now did, felt supported by King and his nurses. His standards and methods seeped through the new suburbs and country towns. They adapted readily to hospitals and orphanages and missions.

Truby King's was a scientific system of child-rearing which, he claimed, would help the New

World escape the tragic decline of the Old. Here was the solution to the danger of declining standards, to the 'Irishness' of large untidy households, to the threat of 'going bush' or worse still, 'native', the fear of new generations who spoke badly. Here too was a systematic methodology for rearing infants that dovetailed neatly with the State's determination to regulate and eventually assimilate 'mixed blood'. His is the language of the white-coated male expert of his day – firm, judgemental, all-knowing. The words he used convey control and hierarchy. Maternal instinct is not to be trusted – nor would it produce little citizens who would be 'self-reliant, self-regulating, moral, obedient, fit, and under complete self-control'.

Truby King mothers and nurses were instructed firmly in managing the baby's will, in how to avoid the child *ruling the roost*, *getting on top of her*, *breaking the rules*. 'Fond and foolish over-indulgence, mismanagement, and spoiling may be as harmful to an infant as callous neglect or intentional cruelty.' Cuddling in between feeds was firmly discouraged; better left to a special hour in the afternoons. For the child's own good, anxious mothers were told, babies must be fed by the clock and allowed to cry if it was not the appointed hour to pick them up.

Indulgence meant denying a child the most important lesson of life, self-discipline. Good habits formed in childhood meant better citizens in a chaotic world.[2]

And of course it was all of a piece. The world was chaotic. People were hungry. Children waited in camps and Homes to come to kindly Australia.

The maps in the newspapers showed borders changing around countries my parents and most people they knew had never visited. They depended on the ABC news, the BBC world service at 9 p.m., the *Age* and the *Argus* with their six-inch headlines. *Hitler Invades Belgium, London Ablaze, Japs in Sydney Harbour.* Reading the newspapers now with expectations of extensive, if inadequate, coverage, they are shocking in their perfunctoriness. There's a kind of oblivion coupled with something deeply unexamined at the heart of the place. But with their lofty yet amateurish voices, few bylines, fewer opinion pieces, the papers sound more representative, more like journals of record, than perhaps they were. So little real information is provided – but I have only other people's memories to rely on, and the newspapers themselves.

Until the photographs of the camps and the horrors of Nuremberg were published after the war, we are told, only a fragmented and dim awareness was possible. The *Argus* in May 1945 gives exactly five centimetres on its back page to the first mention of the capture of Dachau by the US 7th Army: 'They found 50 railway trucks laden with bodies. About 2000 prisoners were liberated.'

Twice as much space is allotted to the account of the 'Widow who still loves her first husband', a soldier reportedly killed two years before and recently discovered in a Rangoon hospital. A double-page spread in the women's pages gives detailed instructions for making-over tired costumes with ric-rac and embroidery, and Noel Coward's *Blithe Spirit* is playing at the Comedy.

People wanted to do the right thing. God was in his heaven and the King and Queen and little Princesses in their fawn overcoats, like I wore, were in London which we knew was in ruins. My small girl's war had consisted of lost ration books and crayon scribbles around fat black newspaper headlines. We were told that our post-war butter ration was three times larger than that of a British family. There were food parcels sewn into white sheeting and addressed with black India ink to great-aunts in Bath, fruit cakes and milk powder tins full of dripping. We would walk to the post office in the main street with my baby brother in the cream cane pram.

The well-modulated words we heard on Sundays, the readings from the Bible and the Book of Common Prayer, were full of sorrow for a cruel and wicked world. The *manifold sins and wickednesses* had always been there, hovering like a dark cloud on the edge of the world – but God's mercy was infinite if we believed in Him, and *the Grace of God which passeth all understanding* would follow us out of the church and hold us safe.

Those who didn't get enough to eat, who couldn't

read or write, who didn't have warm beds to curl up in at night, needed our pity and our kindness. At Sunday School, we made models of mia-mias by billabongs from brown plasticine and dry grass, scattering plum blossoms for water lilies on green poster paint. Here we placed in our imagination the children we saw standing in rows in neat dresses and ankle socks in the photographs from Groote Eylandt and Roper River Mission in the Northern Territory that were pinned up in the Sunday School. We filled our cardboard money boxes with pennies for the good work of the missionaries and, once, a carefully printed letter came back saying thank you. Then someone showed us a home movie of tribal dancing, children playing cricket and tunnel ball and waving thin brown arms at departing cars.

We were attached by the umbilical cord of race and culture at the bottom of the world. Buttressed by older creeds and symbols, the words themselves carried assumptions that are hard to bear. Some of the things we now take for granted had no words at all. Then, culture could only be acquired in museums and from visits overseas. Then, civilization meant not primitive. Assimilation meant the denial of difference. Equality meant being the same. Duty and charity led to salvation. The Aboriginal race was dying out and its remnants would be redeemed by the good works of white people. Then, race was a science: half-caste, quarter-caste, octoroon. And jokes were made about my skinny legs and sunburnt back each summer: *a touch of the tar.*

We lived at the foot of the mountains outside Melbourne, in an old and ramshackle house even by the standards of the early fifties – with deep stone sinks and a wood stove which my mother supplemented with a pressure cooker and a primus. A briquette heater roared above the bath and jets of boiling water blurted onto dirty knees. There was no heating except for open fireplaces and my hands are scarred by chilblains still. But there was panelling and dark polished floors of jarrah, bookcases in every room, a wide verandah that we lived on in summer, an oak tree to climb and private places everywhere.

Under the house on a pile of cushions was where I went to read. They were the books you'd expect: *Little Women, Alice in Wonderland, Swallows and Amazons, The Wind in the Willows, Black Beauty, The Secret Garden,* W.H. Ainsworth's *The Tower of London.* Many were Victorian and Edwardian, much-mended and shipped out to Australia in tin trunks and wooden boxes. There were books with engravings and decorative borders, with pictures of girls with angelic faces kneeling at windows overlooking snow-capped mountains. Their mysterious places were priest holes, gloomy pine forests, gardens with high stone walls. George MacDonald's *The Princess and the Goblin* I knew almost by heart. A little princess, lost and frightened of the dark, finds, at the top of the stairs, a beautiful great-great-great-grandmother spinning a special thread in the moonlight. Whenever the child needs it, the thread will be there in her hand, guiding her past toeless goblins in underground caves to the light high in the window. As the eldest child in my family I was allowed to write my name and the date carefully in ink on the inside cover like the children before me, after my mother and her mother and her mother's mother had done.

The number of new children's authors finding publishers for their work until the mid-fifties was very few. There was little attempt to entice children with futurist fantasies or a sense of their own times. I was the proud owner of the first Puffin, *Worzel Gummidge* by Barbara Euphan Todd, about a scarecrow in an English field with a mangel-worzel for a head.

On my seventh birthday, an anthology was ordered from a London bookshop by my grandmother. *The Patchwork Book*, printed on 'war economy standard' paper, included long extracts from *Coral Island*, *Marco Polo*, Herodotus' description of King Rhampsinitus' Treasure House, Malory's tale of King Arthur and Excalibur, the Story of Kaspar Hauser and deeply affecting Victorian poems of child labour in the mines and chimney stacks of England and Wales. Most extracts would now be rejected by publishers and teachers as too difficult, too 'historical', for young children. There was no 'targeted reading level' or recommended age group, the vocabulary was often beyond my reach but it didn't matter. My reading was as far removed as it was possible to be from the life of a young Australian family on the edge of the bush in a country beginning to re-invent itself. Any disjuncture between the world outside the window and the stories that were so vivid to me in books I never questioned and entered them both as my own.

A similar time-lag existed in the school readers, first published twenty years earlier in 1930 and not yet updated. Illustrations showed mothers in cloche hats and fathers with watchchains across their waistcoats. But the stories and poems were firmly located in the southern hemisphere. Apart from Robbie Burns' 'My Heart's in the Highlands, not here', some Brothers Grimm and Robert Louis Stevenson, an English story about poor children making good through hard work, a couple of Greek legends and one story about a Japanese boy, Yoshi San and O Kiku, his sister, the rest of the world was barely mentioned in Grades 1 to 4.

The Australian bush was full of the terrors that had begun with the frontier society: lost children, bush-fires, drought and shipwrecks. Attacks by snakes and dingoes and crocodiles were survived only by the intervention of friendly blacks speaking pidgin, grateful for occasional rewards of plugs of tobacco. Mrs Aeneas Gunn and Mrs Langloh Parker retold Aboriginal 'legendary tales' and we recited Mary Gilmore's 'The Lost Tribes' with deep solemnity:

Never again from the night, the night that has taken,
Shall ever the tribes return to tell their tale . . .

In so many of the stories, the emphasis is on an
Australian dislike of fuss and praise. There was Simpson
and his Donkey from the First World War, and the
story of Grace Bussell who, with her unnamed black
servant, received the Royal Humane Society's Medal
in 1878 for saving dozens of shipwrecked people from
the surf. The message that is reinforced in story after
story is that Australian children should be courageous
yet self-effacing, self-reliant and kindly, and take matters, including the future, into their own hands.

Many of us in those far-off pre-television days
became 'bookworms' and proud of the state the word
implied. We had our special reading places. We read
on the way home walking along bush tracks and trip-
ping over tree roots. We joined the library next to the
Hall. Our reading shut out the world. We sought
other children with whole sets of favourite authors,
which we devoured on each other's beds at weekends.
Many of these authors my mother made it clear to me
she disapproved of because, she said, the writing was
poor, the authors American or, worse still, Australian.
But I may be doing her a disservice. Certainly I
missed out on *The Magic Pudding* and read only bits of
May Gibbs' *Snugglepot and Cuddlepie* at the library. I
registered her disappointment when she found I was
reading Enid Blyton, or *tripe* – her word for the
fashionable Johanna Spyri *Heidi* books. Her disapproval didn't stop me reading them and nor did she

ever insist. But my mother – a much-loved teacher of other people's children – instilled in me at an early age a recognition that some writing was more worth reading than others.

Two Australian children's authors, Ethel Turner and Mary Grant Bruce, were encouraged, probably because they had engaged my mother's imagination at the same age. *Seven Little Australians*, *The Family at Misrule* and *Mother's Little Girl* were tragic enough for my taste. The Billabong books with their bush fires and shearing sheds, loyal Aboriginal stockmen, and romanticized squattocracy were not the world of the battler or small selector back from the Great War. The Linton family were a limited bunch, the boys like the inarticulate private schoolboys I was to encounter later at university – firm of jaw, good in an emergency, but embarrassed by conversation about worlds outside their own. The girls were splendid, upright and slender, eager to leave the breakfast table where their beautiful mothers presided, to leap into the saddle and follow the muster with the men. But at night they came downstairs, transformed in muslin dresses, hair arranged carelessly in front of smoky mirrors.

My grandmother would have approved.

The Good Neighbour Councils were hard at work in the early fifties welcoming to the district the Dutch

and 'the Balts', attracted to the place presumably for
the same reasons my parents had been. Croydon in
the foothills of the Dandenongs was still rural, land
was cheap and gardens full of liquidambars and rhododendrons. There was work nearby and trains to the
rest of the world every hour. Pamphlets arrived in
letter-boxes telling people *How to Help Someone
Become an Australian Citizen*.

Australia was the safest place on earth and New
Australians, we were told, were lucky to come here,
able to start again and put the past behind them. The
children of recent immigrants arrived at State School
No. 2900 with much better handwriting and language skills than we had. We sensed that they had had
a hard time but we did not ask. Teachers encouraged
the newcomers in our midst to bring their national dress,
to sing their folk songs and to dance for us in front of
the blackboard. We squirmed with sympathy for the
boys with their straight backs and red cheeks and the
girls in full skirts and wooden clogs that drummed
loudly on the wooden floor.

Soon children were three to a desk in Grades 3 and
4 and temporary classrooms were curtained off in a
nearby church hall. There were no high schools this
far from the city for older children, who either left or
travelled long distances on the train to the inner suburbs. By 1951 parents were being canvassed to
support plans to build a new 'model school' for girls
on fifty-two acres of bushland nearby.

'The future of the world rests with the children of
the present and coming generations. If they can be

brought up to appreciate the beauties of the world around them, and the values of life lived in accordance with the teachings of Christ, they will not allow the terrors of war to ruin and destroy mankind,' declared the brochures. Illustrations showed schoolgirls in pigtails feeding calves at the school farm while older girls with books under their arms talked companionably beside picture windows.

I longed to join them.

Somehow my parents scraped together the 'rebatable donation for the building appeal' and I was enrolled. This gave my mother the excuse she was looking for to return to teaching. My father's slow climb up through the various levels of the English, Scottish and Australian Bank which he'd joined early in the Depression, aged sixteen, did not pay enough for school fees. The Education Department did not employ married women, nor did most people approve of them teaching, but my mother found a small family-owned school nearby where she enrolled her third child, my youngest brother, in the kindergarten and gladly returned to teaching for the rest of her working life.

Tintern had been founded as a Ladies College in 1877 in Hawthorn by a Mrs Emma B. Cook. The plans for the new school, to be a memorial to children who had died in the Battle of Britain and a haven for war orphans, reflected some of the radical post-war ideas about education for girls which staff had collected in Scandinavia, the USA and Britain. There were no war orphans among the twenty or so of us who made up the first Junior School, but we had four years of unusual teaching by a young Englishwoman called Eileen Bates. We worked in small groups of different ages at our own pace, from assignment boxes which led us from poetry to bush walks, from listening to music to composing our own, from weighing clay dug from sides of the dam to making pots. Each day was an adventure. *Go your own way. Don't follow the herd*, she'd say.

Then Miss Bates left 'to be a missionary' and there were rumours of arguments over the school's direction.

Soon after this my schooling became conventional. By the mid-1950s Tintern's brochures and reports to parents were declaring its emphasis was on what were still called 'female subjects'. A fifty-per-cent failure rate in Chemistry and worse in Physics reflected the fact that the sciences and maths were branded as skills young women were unlikely to need. Girls who were gifted in them we thought a bit odd, doomed to a dreary future. There were only four, I recall, doing senior mathematics, physics and chemistry by the time we were selecting subjects for outside examination. I, like most of the others, had dropped them.

Our text books were English. Details of crop rotation in Tudor England, the economy of the Ruhr Valley and the stone construction of cambered roadways in eighteenth-century London remain with me still. Kenneth Slessor's 'Five Bells' is the only Australian poem I recall studying and I don't believe there were any novels or short stories written in Australia or America thought to be good enough for us. But we were shown films of migrants building dam walls in the Snowy Mountains and were taken by bus to inspect soil erosion in South Gippsland.

The model school had become something much more typical of its time and place. In our navy-blue uniforms, stockings and velour hats, we daughters of middle-class Melbourne were swathed in matronly cocoons, with aspirations limited more by the weight of conformity and school spirit than by the women who taught us, most of whom were unmarried, kind and clever. The message the school imparted was that marriage was a calling and that education was important in order to be an intelligent partner for your husband – and to have a suitable career if all else failed.

Some of my contemporaries would go on to Invergowrie to be finished off as gracious wife material, others to the major teaching hospitals to become nurses. Very few would make it to university. The school motto was *Factis Non Verbus*, Deeds Not Words. We knew how to smock a baby's dress and cross-stitch tablecloths. We scrubbed dishcloths on pre-war wooden washboards and table-tops to a state of whiteness we would never see again. And I still know how to make blancmange and perfect mashed potatoes.

A small black-and-white photograph of Albert Namatjira sits in my school album next to a snapshot of my best friend and me playing tennis.

Namatjira is holding a painting of a mountain –
which would have been in the transparent purples
and pinks against the clear blue of the skies he was so
famous for. He is looking straight at the camera. His
painting is held delicately by its edges as if it is still
wet.

My parents could not afford to send me on the
school tour to Central Australia in 1954, but my
friend gave me a photograph taken with her Box
Brownie. Albert Namatjira, Arrente painter from the
Hermannsburg Mission in the MacDonnell Ranges,
is standing beside the bus that has brought the load of
Melbourne schoolgirls to his country.

'These dark-skinned people have a style which has
grown up through the ages,' wrote one of the girls in
the school magazine who had watched Namatjira
paint the mountain in the distance at Hermannsburg.
'Now that they have taken up the brush, their art has
lost much of its crudeness; though the straight lines,
circles, and wavy lines can still be seen . . . Most of
the aborigines over-accentuate the colour of the
Centre, but it may be that they see it in more vivid
tones than the white man . . .'

Namatjira has just returned, I now know, from
Canberra where he attended a State Ball in Kings
Hall, Parliament House, in honour of young Queen
Elizabeth II, visiting Australia after her coronation.
He has toured the eastern states, been mobbed by
socialites at art galleries. Ever since his first solo exhi-
bition in Melbourne at the Athenaeum Gallery in
1938, showings of his paintings in the cities had been

sellouts. Police had to be called in to control the crowds. Lady Huntingfield, wife of the Governor of Victoria, opened the first exhibition. 'Namatjira showed the way forward from the primitive to the civilized,' she said.

Throughout 1954 debate raged in the press about whether or not Namatjira should be declared a ward under Section 14 of the Northern Territories Welfare ordinance. Here was a miracle, a gifted artist from an Aboriginal mission. There was public outrage at the conditions he lived in, denied as were the rest of his people the rights of full citizenship. 'Raw deal for top Abo painter!' the Melbourne *Truth* shouted.

Namatjira, 'a wanderer between two worlds', as the papers liked to describe him, died of a heart attack a few years later. He had been sentenced to gaol at Papunya for supplying grog to a family member, in spite of a huge campaign by writers and artists and many other people appalled by the law's rigidity, and the scientific racism it enshrined. 'His humiliation is our humiliation,' wrote painter Noel Counihan in 1958.[3]

Like others of their generation, my parents never discussed with us how they voted and they made jokes for our benefit about not telling each other. Voting was a matter of conscience and a private affair. My father loathed Menzies for reasons to do with his pomposity at least as much as his politics which he didn't admire much either. 'Turn off that coot,' he would say whenever Menzies came on the wireless. Evatt wasn't much better. My father sometimes quoted Walter Murdoch when people intoned that the place was going to the dogs. 'I've always been rather fond of dogs,' Murdoch had written in one of his columns in the *Argus*.

But Australian democracy and its symbols meant much and we were instructed accordingly. Compulsory voting was something to be proud of. Election Day was a big event and we were allowed to sit up listening to the results coming in, as we were during the test cricket – which mattered at least as much as politics.

In the 1950s there was still a lot of 'Englishness' around – not only in my family, which divided down the middle over the Queen, the cricket, standing for the national anthem and the loyal toast on Christmas Day. Family stories mocked the differences and eased the tension. Some of my parents' friends spoke of England as 'home' which we thought pretty silly. There'd be slide nights at the church, privately derided but attended because they raised money for some good cause – endless images of thatched cottages and beef-eaters and stained-glass windows. Our reality was different in the weatherboard hall with the door open on to the bush and the summer night outside.

And in any case, an imaginary England would soon be utterly submerged for me and my friends by American film stars and rock 'n' roll. We pinned our hair into bangs like bobby-soxers – and pored over photographs in magazines of girls in check shirts and

jeans, with small waists and dog collar belts, beside
boys with crewcuts in convertible cars. A school
friend came from a house with a dream kitchen
where we'd make milkshakes after school in the
Mixmaster and drink them perched on stools at
the laminex breakfast bar. I was forbidden to see *Rock
Around the Clock* at the age of fifteen, and the hit
parades on the wireless were firmly turned down, but
under my bed I had my father's wind-up gramo-
phone and 78rpm recordings of pre-war American
jazz and dance music. Sitting on the floor so I could
keep turning the handle and replacing the needles,
the smoky sounds of Fats Waller, Louis Armstrong
and Billie Holiday filled my head.

The idea that we might turn out to be a generation
determined to sit in judgement on our parents, cen-
sor their words and dismiss their codes and
certainties, had not yet dawned on them or on us.
Teenagers were still being invented, sociologists had
not yet started analysing bodgies and widgies, and
respectability hung in the air like a shroud.

The words *ladylike* and *common* still had meaning.
Chaste was what you were expected to be. Mothers
took daughters to corset salons for white cotton bras
and step-ins made of strong elastic with suspenders
attached. Unconfined buttocks were dangerously
inviting. Lipstick for special occasions was a pale

smudge of Yardley Natural Rose removed by Pond's Cold Cream at night. Tampons were for girls who went all the way. The rest of us who didn't, and wore our gloves on the train, were expected to do nothing to get ourselves talked about. We pulled our skirts over our knees, and were told by teachers not to run and jump and laugh too loudly. We tried to rein ourselves in.

But I had a grandmother who delighted in breaking the rules and who carried a hipflask. I had a mother for whom books were a necessity and who went to work. And a father who bought an ancient Austin 7 long after most of the other fathers we knew were paying off new Ford Zephyrs and Holdens. He painted it bright red, drove it with the hood down, and pushed it up the hill most evenings.

The women in my family were linked by books as much as by letter. 'What are you reading?' was almost the first question asked. Books passed back and forth across Bass Strait between my mother and my grandmother and then sometimes to me on the simple principle that if they had enjoyed an author I would also. This usually worked – Virginia Woolf's *Orlando* led me to *The Voyage Out*, Josephine Tey's *The Franchise Affair* to the *The Daughter of Time* and George Orwell's *Animal Farm* and Graham Greene's *Brighton Rock* to everything else of theirs I could find.

But it was the surreptitious reading that left most of a mark. Books considered unsuitable were hidden in parents' wardrobes or covered in brown paper and kept out of reach. We knew where they were in each other's houses, and babysitting other people's children meant being free to roam through descriptions of the unimaginable. Van de Velde's *Ideal Marriage* was easy to spot. A friend of my father didn't know we knew that he had two large volumes, with engravings, of *The Kama Sutra* and *The Decameron*. Australia's censorship laws were all pervasive, with the larger libraries holding copies of banned books 'for legitimate study only' in special collections and requiring letters of authority before they could be referred to. But Henry Miller's *Tropic of Capricorn* and *Tropic of Cancer*, and copies of Anaïs Nin's stories were on some people's shelves, probably having been smuggled in from the States in dustjackets belonging to something else. We read *Lady Chatterley's Lover* which was banned until the mid-sixties, and *Naked Lunch* and *The Story of 'O'* were being passed around in my last years of school.

We read as much for information as for titillation, I think. There was an air of frankness and modernity about most things but little real talk of sexual matters in families like mine. 'Father and son' nights were dutifully attended by my father with my eldest brother. My youngest brother was given a book. My mother was probably relieved I read so much because it saved her from trying to find ways to talk to me about sexual feelings. Instead she gave me Colette's *Chéri* and

Simone de Beauvoir's *The History of Sex* and, when I was about fourteen, Ruth Park's *The Harp in the South*.

Park's first novel had been published by Angus & Robertson in 1948 and had reprinted steadily ever since. Re-reading it now, I can see how it made such an impact on me. Set in Sydney's Surry Hills and Redfern, it brought together the threads of romantic love, working-class life and post-war refugees. Her streets were like the slum streets I'd been driven through in Melbourne's Fitzroy and Collingwood, much of it still unsewered in the 1950s with many families still dependent on an outside tap above a gully trap. The inner suburbs seemed dark and menacing and the message we had absorbed well was how fortunate we were not to have to live like that.

Ruth Park's novel punctured the sense of us and them. Her slums are full of families from everywhere: Australian working-class battlers who may never find the means to escape, Irish immigrants, Jewish refugees, Sicilians – a community held together by the Catholic Church and by people looking out for each other, only too aware of the traumas many of them were struggling to live with. People without hope, some of them, others determined to make good. The horror of Roie Darcy's attempted backyard abortion and her miscarriage at home with her mother lay just below the surface of the happy ending. By then Roie had fallen in love with Charlie Rothe, a part Aboriginal accepted without question by the family because they loved each other.

She woke quietly, opening her eyes suddenly on the bright, light room with the sea-dapple sliding over the ceiling. She turned her head, and right under her lips was Charlie's warm soft hair. His head was on her shoulder, his arm flung across her, one knee over hers . . . His dark blood was plain now, but it gave to his face an exotic difference in the line of his lips and the triangularity of his eyebrows. He was hers and she his; the mystery had been consummated.[4]

Then my family moved to the country. And the romance of childhood – in the untidy old house at the foot of the mountains, with the bush over the road, the white wooden church and the trainline to the rest of the world – came to an end.

In preparation for a city branch, my father was sent for a few years' country experience first to Coleraine near the South Australian border and then to Colac, west of Melbourne in the heart of the ancient volcanic landscape and the basalt plains. Here he would get to know the remnants of the old Western District families, their accounts fat from the wool boom. And there were the new bank customers, the Italian crop farmers in the Stoney Rises, with their drystone walls against the rabbits, their homemade salamis and grappa, which they'd press on my father, and whose children my mother would teach to read in English at the consolidated school.

My matriculation year was to have been in the much-imagined model boarding school with the picture windows. But by now I was in deep rebellion against Deeds Not Words, and all that it then stood for. A few days before first term began, I decided to enrol myself at the local high school.

I joined the matriculation class at Colac High in 1958. The school was in an old brick building on the main highway out of town, and the windows rattled each time the trucks thundered past. There was a muddy oval and a great deal of cracked asphalt where we lined up whatever the weather to salute the flag and honour the Queen. Our tunics were shiny with badly pressed pleats, socks an unflattering navy blue, but the two boys and four girls in their final year were taught with a mix of correspondence classes and tutorials that suited me down to the ground.

It was in Matriculation that I first studied Australian history, still called British History, from several general texts and from Manning Clark's *Select Documents in Australian History*, which, in its grey covers and dull design, looked more like a manual of mechanical engineering than something intended to engage young readers.

My mind made no connection to the fact that the miners' uprising at the Eureka Stockade took place a few miles to the north near Ballarat; nor that many of the surrounding mountain peaks in the local landscape had been named for Classical Antiquity by explorer Major Mitchell; nor that nearby at Barwon Park, Thomas Austin, pastoralist and sportsman, had imported twenty-four wild rabbits in 1859 to satisfy the urges of his English guests. So well did the rabbits acclimatize that between 1871 and 1886 the Western Meat Preserving Company at Colac canned 6.5 million of them, most for export back to Britain.[5]

Australian history was not real history and, in any case, I was too engrossed in the nineteenth-century novels and the romantic poets we were reading to pay much attention. Adrienne Walker, just out of teacher's college, wore her hair in a knot like the heroines of the books she sometimes read aloud to us. 'To be loved to madness – such was her great desire . . . A blaze of love, and extinction, was better than a lantern glimmer of the same which should last long years.'[6] Miss Walker persevered with red cheeks, her voice firm, despite the boys' groans.

Thomas Hardy's ideal of love and the romantic poets and novels came alive for me in the dark classroom that smelt of kerosene heater and damp wool. Inside the cover of my copy of *The Return of the Native* from that year, I found a note I'd written to myself: 'The characters which survive are those who make some compromise with their surroundings.'

2

'A Creative Phase'

My room was in a different shabby Carlton terrace house each year I was at university, and my books went with me. My dismayed father would help me lug the boxes up and down dark staircases which smelt of cabbage and tobacco – the smell of the slums and the Depression to him, I now realize. Then, I thought he was ashamed of a daughter who didn't want the usual solution of living at home or in college, and that he was only too aware of the freedom those rooms meant to me. I'd arrange my books on planks propped up with bricks, position my reading light, set the rest of the scene with cushions, a mattress, posters and a square of seagrass matting, and my year would begin.

In the early 1960s, Melbourne University, like all Australian universities, was still steeped in the orthodoxies of Cambridge and Oxford, reminding those who needed reminding that great literature, like all great things, came from the Old World. Leavis was

God. The canon was immutable. And the eighteen novels read during the first- and second-year honours course in English Language and Literature ranged in deference to the Great Tradition from Defoe's *Moll Flanders* to Lawrence's *The Rainbow*.

We read *Middlemarch*, *Crime and Punishment*, *Wuthering Heights*, *Emma*, *The Scarlet Letter*, *Portrait of a Lady*, *A Portrait of the Artist as a Young Man* and many others. We had the luxury of spending a whole term on *The Waste Land* and to explore, tentatively, Eliot's footnotes – the *Upanishads*, the *Bhagavad Gita*, the Gospels, Dante. The poets ranged from Spenser and Chaucer to Auden. We read Plato, Homer, *Beowulf*, *Njal's Saga*, *Aucassin and Nicolette* and in first-year French we were expected to read, in French, *Le Rouge et le Noir*, *Madame Bovary*, *Germinal*, Victor Hugo, Molière. In History there was Tawney and Collingwood, Francis Bacon, Machiavelli and John Stuart Mill.

There were few women, of course, fewer Americans or even Russians, and no colonials. Contemporary writers would have to wait their turn. It seemed to take at least three generations before a writer could be confidently declared to have what it took *to last*. Those writers whose *distinctive creative genius* set them apart from all others, we were expected to accept and simply redefine their formal perfection of construction. The difference between *sustained seriousness* and *entertainment*, the hierarchy of major and minor works, was never far from the surface. And many of the lectures seemed to me then, and at this distance, more set on

ranking and dissecting than on broadening our understanding and appreciation of the works.

Now, when I return to some of the books, my
seventeen- and eighteen-year-old self rises up to greet
me – craving a level of enlightenment that was fairly
hard to satisfy, easily bored, always wanting more but
not knowing what it was I sought.

A passion for the stoics – or rather for the classics
student who read me Catullus and Virgil – is there in
a volume I have still of A.F.L. Farquharson's translation of Marcus Aurelius' *Meditations*. When I open
the book in its battered green dustjacket, there are
pine needles from Mt Macedon pressed inside and a
card in Latin, *Anno* MCMLXI. My friend's pleasure
was to drive out of town in his mother's two-toned
Holden EH to a pine forest on a hillside which
reflected the classical settings of the poems. These he
read me first in Latin and again in translation, footnotes and all. My pleasure was to watch him and to
listen to his voice. Inevitably my stoicism was spotted
for the fraud it was and he left for an archaeological
dig in Turkey.

For a time, I wrote bad poetry about Lydian cav-
alry and 'moon-bleached bones', and played over and
over again late at night Alfred Deller singing the
Agnus Dei from Bach's *Mass in B minor*. I went to
Mass in Parkville for nearly a year, sitting at the back
hoping to be taken in, religious and romantic yearn-
ings curiously entwined. My missal, printed in lovely
round Garamond type in red and black, still sits on
the shelf next to Marcus Aurelius.

But sometimes – mainly in tutorials which seem in memory to have been held always in smoke-filled rooms on winter's mornings with the sun streaming in through the lead-lighted windows of the Old Arts building – there were performances, readings, a visible delight in language which got to me and lasted. Vincent Buckley reading Yeats' 'The Wild Swans at Coole' with Irish rhythm, Gay Tennant, chainsmoking in her wheelchair, taking us lovingly and fiercely through the pounding wordshapes of Gerard Manley Hopkins, or Ian Maxwell reciting rolling gusts of *Beowulf* to the small honours tutorial – we were privileged and we knew it. The English Department in the early sixties had at least four published poets as tutors and lecturers. Philip Martin, Evan Jones, Chris Wallace-Crabbe and Vin Buckley with faces alight read us the work of other poets at least as much for the pleasure of it as for our instruction. Buckley, a poet whose own work I later cherished, was one of those teachers who believed that the first task always was *to present the work*, and I began to think about the shapes and sounds of words and their layered meanings.

I was an impatient student, changing subjects, torn between student theatre and the occasional surge of delight in study which hinted at the existence somewhere of an intellectual life. By third year, full of hope, I switched from a combined degree to a History major. But the History department had seen better days. Max Crawford, legendary teacher and Head of Department who had been appointed as a young man from Sydney in the late thirties and transformed the teaching of history, was ill and remote. Manning Clark, who had first established Australian History there in 1948, was long since gone to the Australian National University. In retrospect it was bad timing.

Then I found myself wanting.

The History Department was firmly of the empirical school with the past knowable only through the examinable evidence it had left. Historical documents were artefacts. Some issues were worth studying, others were not. Some subjects were not only beyond our reach, but were regarded with suspicion, disdained as lightweight, lacking in rigour. Ian Robertson illuminated the Italian Renaissance and in Kathleen Fitzpatrick's hands, the discipline of British History rose to heights of eloquence; in other hands it sometimes felt like fact-grubbing.

To me, though obviously not to everyone, some of whom went on to become distinguished teachers of history themselves, the emphasis on evidence often came at the expense of imagination. My curiosity about the Levellers was shortlived and my hopeless attempts at long distance to interpret the jewelled purse lid and buckles discovered in the burial mound at Sutton Hoo, near Woodbridge in Suffolk, were frustrated by the fact that I'd only seen them in poor black-and-white photographs. Colour, it seemed, was considered rather dubious by the History and the Fine Arts departments. So were my attempts to imagine the wearers of the buckles in the context of the sagas we read in Old English.

Whenever I was drawn by a sequence that failed to fit, and struggled to put into words what I was trying to think about, I was pulled up as if I had crossed some line that I didn't understand. Margaret Kiddle's study of Western District squatters, *Men of Yesterday*, was published in 1961. Her work was much admired but her approach to social history and her engagement with her evidence in order to elucidate seemed to be the exception and to have left little trace on the teachings of the department. Nor were sociology, anthropology, ethnography or psychology then seen as having much to offer. 'This is the stuff of American paperbacks,' reprimanded a supervisor when I submitted a thesis topic on the meanings of pagan and early Christian imagery in the Lindisfarne Gospels. Of course it would have been far too difficult. I would have had to make things up, venture far from the facts, imagine as well as demonstrate.

There was, until my final year in 1964 when I would discover Pacific Prehistory, a complete absence of Australian subjects in my choice of courses. Only a handful of post-war Australian writers made it into the prescribed reading lists of the Arts Faculty by the early sixties. Bernard Smith and Robin Boyd were studied in Fine Arts. Australian History, a rather lowly one-year option alongside American and Far Eastern History, drew on Manning Clark's *Select Documents in Australian History*, Brian Fitzpatrick's *The Australian People* and Vance Palmer's *The Legend of the Nineties*. Australian Literature was an optional third-year honours subject which I would avoid in my ignorance and so failed to encounter Judith Wright's great poems in *The Moving Image* and *Woman to Man*, Xavier Herbert's *Capricornia*, Martin Boyd's *The Cardboard Crown* and Patrick White's *Voss*.

I was too immersed in European history and literature and student theatre to regard a year of what the handbook described 'the study of Australian literature and certain aspects of Australian cultural history' as having anything remotely interesting enough to offer me.

My real university life seems to have been backstage at the Union theatre, sewing sequins on cloaks, painting sets all night, immersed in productions of revues, discussing and rehearsing the European modernists, acting whenever I could. I played Emilia in *Othello* and one of Genet's maids. I played Catharine in Tennessee Williams' *Suddenly Last Summer* and survived the scorn of the *Farrago* drama critic who declared that my homemade suit 'could not by any stretch of the imagination have come from Paris'. We staged with the Sydney University Dramatic Society an ambitious season of Theatre of the Absurd which included playwrights such as Jarry, Ionesco, Beckett, Cocteau, Arrabal, Genet.

One day I had to leave a rehearsal of *The Maids* for a job interview, and trailed over to the terrace house with the bow window in Royal Parade, Parkville,

where *Meanjin* was housed. Part-time work was not
approved of for the small group of honours students
of which I was still managing to be part, but a few
half days a week at a literary magazine I'd only dimly
heard of would pay for my room and my books. The
Commonwealth Scholarship Scheme paid for my fees.

The editor, Clem Christesen, had put the word out
that he needed some occasional student help with the
magazine. I'd been warned that he was formidable and
could be fierce but instead I was welcomed. Christesen
looked to me rather dashing – like a Hollywood
character out of a Chicago newspaper office – pacing
the floor, puffing his Craven A cigarettes, as he
described what small magazines were all about, and
what he was trying to do with this one that he had
begun in Brisbane during the war years. He demanded
to know what I was reading – and I can't recall what I
answered – but he showed me a Patrick White story,
'Down at the Dump', which had just come in, the first
White had sent to the magazine.[1]

There was no mention of my typing – invariably a
key question asked of women then – or of what I was
expected to do or how I'd be paid.

I would like to be able to say that the book-lined
offices of *Meanjin,* with the Louis Kahan drawings of
writers and the paintings by Jock Frater and Lina
Bryans on the walls, impressed me mightily, and that I
left that afternoon knowing in my bones that I'd landed
a job with a literary magazine that would, in some
ways, begin to define the way I would work for many
years. But of course I didn't. I doubt I understood that

I would be working at a place that was encouraging Australian writers by giving them somewhere to publish their essays and poems and short stories, an opportunity that, except in a handful of other small magazines and one or two publishing houses, hardly existed elsewhere.

For the next two years for a few hours each week, paid somewhat erratically in pound notes out of the editor's green petty cash box in the filing cabinet, I sat at a desk looking out on to the elm trees in Royal Parade, surrounded by subscription cards, filling in records and addressing envelopes. I was desperately bored unless I was reading or writing something or able to listen in to the conversations in the next room. To *Meanjin* came real writers: Dorothy Green, Judith Wright, Brian Fitzpatrick, Patrick White, A.A. Phillips, David Martin, A.D. Hope, all climbed the steep stairs to the first-floor offices during my time there, bringing contributions for the magazine or because they were visiting Melbourne. I'd heard of few of them and read almost nothing of their work but I was allowed to borrow books from the *Meanjin* shelves.

Meanjin's office was a writers' centre of the day, full of cigarette and pipe smoke, where bottles of red wine were opened sometimes in the late afternoons and the talk flowed. It was the kind of talk I hadn't been hearing at Melbourne University, passionate talk about writing and criticism, politics and place. The political was tangible and the arguments very different from the fuzziness of my kind of student politics at that time. I had been temporarily galvanized by apartheid in South Africa, demonstrations against the White Australia Policy in 1960 and in support of Abschol, the Aboriginal Scholarship scheme the following year, but nothing else had sent us out of the theatre to march down Swanston Street to Parliament House.

The issues were larger and were somehow more real overseas. Or so it seemed to me. Canberra was a dun-coloured stage set for events too dreary for notice. Kennedy was in the White House and the Cuban missile crisis had begun. The Berlin Wall had been built in 1961, Eichmann was found guilty and hanged the following year. The race riots in Birmingham, Alabama, and the arrest of Martin Luther King felt more immediate and had more impact on me than the abysmal state of our own race relations which were invisible in the cities if you didn't know where to look. They rarely made headlines and we had to force ourselves to think about them.

Australia's involvement in Vietnam was still three years away. So was a belief in the revolutionary power of small presses to change the world. We were reading *Cahiers du Cinema* and queuing for the latest films of Pasolini, Bergman, Truffaut, Antonioni. We read Australian magazines such as *Nation* and the *Observer* and sometimes the new *Dissent* in the library but the idea that there might be a shift in consciousness, the start of a postcolonial perspective finding the words to shape itself on the edge of the campus hadn't occurred to me.

Australia was still locked in the Cold War and

Meanjin was publishing in opposition to the prevailing political climate. Clem and Nina Christesen's visits to Moscow and their inclusion in the magazine of poets such as Yevgeny Yevtushenko and Bella Akhmadulina and short story writers in translation were acts seen as determinedly provocative in some quarters. Nina Christesen, as founder and head of the Russian Department at Melbourne University and Clem, as editor of *Meanjin*, visited Russia on separate occasions. The fear that 'politics' would jeopardize the university's relationship with the magazine was a constant concern.[2]

When *Meanjin* had moved to Melbourne University in 1945, at the university's invitation, Clem Christesen had hoped to find the secure base all small magazines need and the academic standing he believed was warranted for himself as editor and founder. Neither happened. Instead he was embattled. *Meanjin* had its loyal supporters who argued for it but the minutes of the Lockie Bequest meetings reflect institutional irritation and incomprehension of the magazine's charter, most often expressed by the university's Registrar. Christesen was publishing a radical little magazine into a market that barely existed beyond a largely oblivious academy and a literary world that was at times both anti-intellectual and deeply conservative. In the eyes of some of the university administrators the magazine was a potential embarrassment at best, a hotbed of dangerous opinions at worst – and it was quite regularly caricatured as such in the press.

At this time only a small number of people at Melbourne University had much sense of many of the riches in their custody. Gwyn James, Manager of Melbourne University Press, was under pressure. The University's art collection, which consisted of some major bequests, was scattered and under-appreciated. The unique autobiographical Grainger Museum, which faced *Meanjin* across Royal Parade, had been bestowed on the university by the composer, but the building, begun in 1935, was still unfinished when Grainger died in 1961. The collection of thousands of photographs, memorabilia, musical instruments, and early recordings, was under regular threat. The museum was open only by special arrangement – and was regarded as a bit of a joke because of its paraphernalia of flagellation. The unpacked crates and the dim lighting made it seem more of a mausoleum than the rich site it has since become. I remember the smell of damp and mould.

Meanjin's finances remained precarious and the editor's 'expenses' rather than a professorial salary must have been humiliating. The Commonwealth Literary Fund and the University's Lockie Bequest were its mainstay, with donations sometimes added by some people to their subscription cheques. Contributors were paid small fees and the basic rate topped up by the editor whenever he could. Authors like Xavier Herbert who, despite the editor's best efforts, still complained, received ferocious letters explaining what Christesen was up against. Some of these have become editorial classics of their kind.

Subscription sales per issue were rather larger than they are now – around 3500, I recall – at least partly because institutional support through libraries and government departments and embassies was far greater. But the concern was always there about the rate of subscriber renewal, and the worst part of my job was having to make phone calls to those who had failed to respond to several reminders.

The magazine then was more than twenty years old and many of the subscribers were loyal but aging; the editor hoped to entice a new generation of readers by making space for younger writers – poetry from David Malouf and Rodney Hall, stories and articles from writers such as Robert Hughes and Frank Moorhouse.

Much of the prose Christesen commissioned and the articles and essays he published then were arguments about the meaning of a strong Australian artistic and cultural life, instead of a literary culture riddled with the disappointment of being here rather than somewhere else, ever anxious to be classed the same, as good as, of the 'first rank'. It was in *Meanjin*, in 1950, that A.A. Phillips had first published his definitive analysis of the cultural cringe – and *Meanjin* continued the debate. The poetry the magazine published was a rich mix of Europeans in translation and Australians such as Rosemary Dobson, A.D. Hope, Gwen Harwood, Judith Wright, Dorothy Auchterlonie (Green), David Campbell, Vincent Buckley and Philip Martin. I read them in the *Meanjin* office for the first time.

Christesen had the shape in his head of the year's four issues and would speak of them as if they already existed. Each day he'd write rapid notes on blue copy paper to contributors he'd commissioned and to those who had sent in unsolicited manuscripts. They were tough and frank, the comments I saw, but constructive. If something about the writing appealed to him, he'd read bits out to whoever happened to be nearby or to the next telephone caller. Sometimes he'd leave me notes attached to manuscripts. 'Needs something more. What do you *think*?' My rudimentary comments were more help to me than to Clem and I doubt he intended to train me. More likely, it was a way of sharing his enthusiasm. He considered that the work of *Meanjin* was of the greatest significance – and what he was achieving began to dawn on me.

I had arrived at *Meanjin* oblivious of Australian literature – but my little job there imprinted on me a sense that editors should be active not passive, that grammar and punctuation and spelling meant much – Christesen was meticulous – but that what was being *said* meant more. He spoke of how no two writers ever wrote a sentence the same way, and how the differences between them must be preserved not flattened out. Pedantry and academic waffle, as he called it, were not welcome in *Meanjin* – balm, I guess, to my rather bruised scholastic sensibilities.

By observing Christesen and reading through his bookshelves I learnt more than I realized about how the magazine was shaped and sent to the printer. The

difference between a manuscript and well designed
and edited pages, how typesetting carries the authority of words ready to be read, how typefaces
themselves convey a range of meanings and how
words read more smoothly when they are spaced
properly – I was gaining a practical knowledge of
typefaces and the 'look' of a page. And I experienced
that particular and visceral pleasure of seeing type-
written words turned into printed pages that *read
well*.

Meanjin was of plain design with generous margins,
set in Baskerville, but with much thought given to
the page layouts, the illustrations – always pen drawings, linocuts and woodcuts, seldom photographs –
and the cover designs commissioned from artists of
the day. I remember from my time there cover paintings and drawings from Aboriginal artists at Yirrkala,
Arthur Boyd, Stanislaw Ostoja-Kotkowski, John
Olsen, Stanislaus Rapotec, Judy Cassab and Fred
Williams.

Then came the moment when advance copies
arrived from the printer, the pleasure of opening
them and smelling their newness, and sharing with
the editor and his secretary, Mamie Smith, all the
hours of the obligatory drudgery stuffing magazines
into labelled envelopes to send them out into the
world.

I learnt enough to begin producing with Jennifer
Murphy a magazine we called – with fashionable
minimalism – *Theatre*. We copied *Meanjin's* production procedures to the letter – somehow persuading

the printer, Fraser and Jenkinson at the top of Queen Street, to give us a student discount, or maybe Clem Christesen did for us. Tate Adams, master print-maker, who was regularly producing his fine linocuts for *Meanjin*, gave me much help with the design of the magazine and several of our theatre programmes. He made original linocuts, and helped persuade the bemused printer to print them on rather avant-garde brown paper. I read and corrected long galley proofs, cut them up into pages, as I'd seen Christesen do, for rough layouts on double page sheets carefully ruled up in blue pencil. I watched as the printer made the pages from the galleys and plates from Tate Adams' linocuts.

Theatre ran for six issues and published some of the luminaries of Sydney and Melbourne student theatre of the day. Paul Eddey, Penelope Curtis, Germaine Greer, Peter Corrigan, Patrick McCaughey, Albie Thoms, Alison Smith, Louise Thorne, Robin Grove – many of them writing articles and reviews that stand re-reading. My two contributions don't. One, about 'Early Melbourne Theatre', at least had me researching the archives of some of the family-owned printers that still existed – firms like Troedel and Cooper with their gorgeously coloured handbills and posters of early productions such as George Durrell's original Australian play, *The Squatter*, a big hit at the Theatre Royal. The theatre had opened in Bourke Street in 1842, was rebuilt to handle the big-spending throngs of the gold rushes and was where Lola Montez would perform her famous Spider

Dance. My other article was a derivative piece about the work of playwrights I had never read and directors I had never seen – Frisch and Hochwaelder, Jouvet and Viertel – in order to hold forth about theatre as 'a communicative medium'.

A sense of an Australian literary tradition as a struggle to be heard, and of the efforts needed by some people to support Australian creativity, I owed to those years as a lowly, part-time, eavesdropping assistant at *Meanjin*. And that portion of my brain I now think of as forever shaped 'editorial' was beginning to work. The other part I kept to myself. But when I was alone in the office, I'd type the beginnings of stories with two fingers on the big *Meanjin* typewriter, which clanged loudly at the end of each line.

In the summer of 1963–4, I was asked to join a small expedition to Koonalda Cave in the Nullarbor Plain before Eucla on the South Australian border. To the north was the railway line running between Adelaide and Perth, its sidings named for prime ministers Deakin, Hughes, Cook, Fisher, and to the south across an arid plain with its purply saltbush, the Great Australian Bight.

There had been expeditions before to the limestone cave. Since 1956 Hungarian *émigré* and archaeologist Alexander Gallus had been excavating

Koonalda whenever he could. We were mainly students recruited to help with the dig and the recording of the finds.

At that time Koonalda Cave was the only known site in the Nullarbor to have signs of human occupation but how old it might be was in dispute. Near the entrance Gallus had already found evidence of the manufacture of flake axes, scrapers, blades and, at the far end of the tunnel, a place where flint nodules had been gouged from the walls.

The cave was in a deep sinkhole on a cattle station belonging to a pioneering family of the Nullarbor. Their house was built of railway sleepers with an earthen floor and surrounded by a yard lined with neat rows of bottles filled with water against the almost permanent drought. There were chooks wandering free and a pen with a wombat in it which would be served up to us for a welcoming dinner one evening – roasted with crackling and an apple in its mouth, accompanied by tinned peas and roast potatoes. There were lots of handsome fair-haired children who thought nothing of driving several hundred kilometres to play tennis on neighbouring cattle stations.

We set up camp a few kilometres to the north on the edge of the sinkhole. Early each morning wearing big boots and helmets and wrapped in warm clothing although the day was already hot, we climbed with a rope down the 60-metre cliff face to the entrance of Koonalda Cave.

This opened on to a long tunnel that went for more than 250 metres under the Nullarbor Plain. As soon as we stepped out of the brilliant glare of light on the limestone rocks at the entrance the cold hit us and the cave floor sloped down in total darkness. Here were deep pools so clear that they were invisible in the light of our carbide lamps. We waded to where the tunnel rose up again then climbed over boulders into a long tight chute we called the Squeeze, with its mysterious cross-hatched markings and handprints.

All day we'd work with brushes on stones half buried in the white limestone dust, numbering and measuring. Then at night we sat around the campfire with the immense dome of the southern sky above us. We conjured up scenes of small bands of people moving across the land. We imagined the lives of those who sheltered in the cave from the sun and the freezing nights, who must have walked into the dark carrying some kind of fire-stick to where they knew was the flint they needed. This moment, magical or practical or both, they marked on the wall.

In the stories of local Aboriginals the caves were believed to have been occupied by people different in every way from themselves and they refused to enter them. Further evidence, we decided, against the theory recently promoted by Cambridge archaeologist, Grahame Clark, in *World Prehistory*[3] and accepted by most Australian fieldworkers and museums, that 'Australia was mainly peopled by a single race . . . possessing highly complex social institutions . . . and first settled a few thousand years ago'. The archaeological map of Australia at this time was officially rather empty.

But Gallus was convinced that the evidence for human occupation in northern Australia would eventually be dated as at least 50,000 years old and in Koonalda Cave in the far south about 30,000 years before the present.[4] The flint artefacts at Koonalda, he said, were, in their typology and use-wear, not unlike the Central European Paleolithic that he was experienced in detecting.

This ancientness was almost unthinkable in 1963. Thirty-eight thousand years before what we knew as Antiquity, when the earth's climate was much colder than it is today, Australia was separated from Asia by a deep and narrow strait of about 80 kilometres making rafts or canoes necessary for any journey. And the people who brought their skills and their beliefs with them must have gradually spread south and west, in hunter-gatherer bands, and developed their distinctive cultures in response to the land. Just trying to think about it anchored me.

Gallus was a Catholic who quoted Jung's theories of the collective unconscious and magical archetypes – and encouraged our reading and our thinking. He had arrived in Australia with a formidable reputation as a Central European archaeologist from the Museum of Budapest, his publications list was impressive, his qualifications acknowledged but ignored. When he sought official support for his fieldwork, his theories were derided and he relied on amateur enthusiasts, students like me, in the summer vacation, to get themselves across the Nullarbor.

Intellectually and methodologically Gallus stood

between the entrenched Cambridge-in-the-bush school of archaeology and the one or two American scholars working in the new field of ethno-archaeological research. The best that could be done, said historian Kathleen Fitzpatrick, was to regard him as having 'unofficial M.A. status'. Gallus probably remained an outsider for the rest of his life.

His difficulties would have owed as much to the undeveloped state of Australian archaeology as to prejudice and bureaucracy. The fourth-year History honours option in Pacific Prehistory taught by John Mulvaney, which I commenced in 1964, was just five years old and offered the only Australian archaeology taught in any university. There was one museum curator in the country with any formal archaeological training. Real archaeology happened elsewhere. In 1960 the oldest dated relics in Australia were 9000 years before the present. Some people did anticipate that human occupation would be found to be older than this but in the early sixties only seventeen sites had been radio-carbon dated. By 1975 there were more than 150.[5]

It is tempting now to see Gallus' story as that of so many Europeans who arrived in Australia in the 1950s, to find themselves marginalized, teaching schoolchildren rather than being welcomed for what they had to offer to a university department. Since then Gallus has been somewhat vindicated. John Mulvaney, who was largely responsible for putting Australian prehistory on the map and filling in many of the blanks, gives Gallus full credit for persistence in the sixties. And dates of up to 40,000 years have since been established for the site.[6]

∽

'My own feeling,' Allen Lane wrote to W.E. Williams in 1961, 'is that Australia is about to emerge, speaking from a publishing point of view, into a creative phase in place of an absorbent one.'[7]

He was right about the creative phase although I didn't know that then. Allen Lane, Penguin founder and Chairman, my grandmother's hero, had been visiting Australia regularly since 1953. His nose for cultural shifts and new ideas was legendary. He travelled constantly between the new companies in the Penguin group, in Baltimore, in Delhi, Melbourne, West Africa, Canada. Bill Williams, later Sir William Emrys Williams, a close friend of Lane who shared his passion for the concept of mass education, and who had launched the Army Bureau of Current Affairs and established the British Institute of Adult Education, was a source of advice and a sounding board during the years of Penguin's greatest expansion.

'I should try to dig in in Australia and India,' Williams had written to Lane in 1947. 'Every conversation I have with intelligent Indians confirms in me the belief that, once they have cast off the political shackles to Great Britain, they will be all the more culturally receptive to us.'[8]

On the other hand, Australia, Lane thought, was at

the beginning of a rather different stage. When visiting the country he talked to writers and artists. Rudy Komon, dealer and wine buff, friend of the painters and sculptors of the day, introduced Lane to Robert Klippel, William Dobell, Russell Drysdale, Fred Williams and Arthur Boyd. He met Patrick White and A.D. Hope, Nugget Coombs, the young Robert Hughes, and many other writers and critics. What Lane was observing was an increased confidence in their own perspective from those engaged in making art and literature.

Nineteen sixty-one was a good year. Patrick White's *Riders in the Chariot* was published to great acclaim in the States and even the *Sydney Morning Herald* reviewer, Charles Higham, praised it highly. White's play, *The Ham Funeral*, opened in Adelaide followed by a sellout Sydney season. Bernard Smith's *European Vision and the South Pacific* and Robin Boyd's *The Australian Ugliness* had just been published and Manning Clark's first volume of his *History of Australia* was about to appear.

Composer Peter Sculthorpe returned in 1961 from Oxford, which 'had sharpened his awareness of things Australian and his feeling that temperamentally he did not belong in England.'[9] His early great works, his *Sun Music* series, *Irkanda I–IV* and his *Sixth String Quartet*, belong to this time. The Australian Ballet Foundation and School was being established with the encouragement of Nugget Coombs under the direction of Peggy van Praagh and Margaret Scott to keep dancers in Australia on a professional basis and enable Australian originated work to be performed.

This was the same message I would start to absorb at *Meanjin* – that more was going on in Australian writing and painting, music and dance than London critics and editors and probably most Australians were able to see.

Allen Lane with his publisher's sixth sense knew this but he also knew that the long 'absorbent' phase he saw coming to an end had suited British publishers well. Some had set up distribution companies many years earlier; some still employed commission agents to sell books direct. The hunger in Australia for books had been remarked upon from the earliest days of the colonies. The long sea voyages, solitary lives led in the bush, the loneliness and melancholia of emigration whether enforced or voluntary – all must have contributed to Australian reading habits. To cater for the demand for the popular books of the day, 'colonial editions' had often been printed throughout the nineteenth century and well into the twentieth on cheaper paper. Authors were paid 'colonial royalties' at about half the rate of the UK home market to reflect the costs of supplying readers at the bottom of the world.[10]

British publishing had high standards and was much sought after. It had a long and lustrous tradition. Most authors would have undoubtedly regarded being published in Australia as second-best. Publication in England meant an author had some chance of being read as an insider rather than as a colonial, but risked their voice or stylistic idiosyncrasies being pronounced as lacking rather than applauded.

Authors whose subject matter or writing style put

them outside the notice of English agents or publishers, had a limited choice of Australian outlets. So did
those in the tradition of the *Bulletin* school and the
social realists of the 1930s who were passionate about
being 'homegrown' and for whom English editorial
procedures were unendurable.

Few Australian writers had British agents. Curtis
Brown did not open its Sydney office until the late
sixties. Authors with aspirations or subject matter
more suited to an English readership somehow
weathered the six-month cycle or more of posting an
unsolicited manuscript by sea mail and waiting for its
almost inevitable return. Editorial advice or rejection
was conveyed by letter, acceptance and terms of offer
by telegram. Australian literary biography is full of
horror stories of slights, condescension, misunderstandings and terse exchanges – and not only with
British publishers, of course. Patrick White and
Christina Stead were published out of New York and
London and their hardcovers imported into Australia.
Stead, after years of receiving a 'colonial royalty' from
publisher Peter Davies for sales of her books in Australia, tried Angus & Robertson with *A Little Tea, A
Little Chat* and received what she considered an
'impudent' reply from A&R editor Colin Roderick.
She was still smarting when she wrote to Nettie
Palmer in 1951:'A&R were offered my first book . . .
by my father . . . about 1924 or 1925 . . . and this
firm has not yet made up its mind to take anything of
mine: and who else is there? I consider it disgraceful,
and that disgrace is not mine.'[11]

How rarely writers would have felt encouraged or supported except by each other and by the editors of small magazines in the way I was observing Clem Christesen doing at *Meanjin*. How few of them would have ever received a cable such as American editor at Viking, Ben Heubsch, sent to Patrick White immediately after reading *The Tree of Man*, on 11 November 1954.

> VIKING CONGRATULATES YOU ON A BEAUTIFUL PROFOUNDLY IMPRESSIVE FULFILMENT OF EXPECTATIONS.[12]

Most Australian authors were forced until a couple of generations ago to seek their primary audience elsewhere, writing out of their Australian experience for readers at the centre which was always somewhere else. A sad kind of mid-Atlantic tone pervades many of the Australian popular novels of this period that were published in England primarily for the library market.

Local critics could be depended on to carp if the overseas reviews were too glowing. A.D. Hope's legendary savaging of *The Tree of Man* in the *Sydney Morning Herald* in 1956 as 'pretentious and illiterate verbal sludge' wounded White deeply, but the final straw might have been the review by Eric Lambert, the Australian novelist on the English *Tribune,* who produced what White described as 'a study in malevolence and frustration' . . .

nothing I have written [according to Lambert] is the least bit Australian, *The Tree of Man* is like a burlesque of D.H. Lawrence by Perelman, the Great Australian Novel has often been written, acclaimed with affection by humble people, and absorbed into the Australian Dream, etc. etc. How sick I am of the bloody word AUSTRALIA. What a pity, I am part of it; if I were not, I would get out tomorrow. As it is, they will have me with them till my bitter end, and there are about six more of my unAustralian Australian novels to fling in their faces . . .[13]

The beginning in 1961 of 'a creative phase' which Lane observed was also the moment when an Australian publishing programme was first mooted at Penguin – where Australian literature and history, current affairs and reference books could be published alongside international titles. Allen Lane responded well to the idea when it was proposed to him by Geoffrey Dutton, Max Harris and the then Australian Managing Director, Brian Stonier. There would be the added benefit of introducing some Australian writers in paperback to English readers, they argued.

English editors in the sixties had little reason to imagine there might be more Australian writing worth reading. The writers themselves and the literary magazines that sustained them knew better, but there was a strong sense in Australia itself that the population was too small to support a genuine literature.

Australian books were sometimes included in series commissioned by British hardback publishers but were regularly panned by English critics. The dismissal that Judith Wright's anthology of Australian poetry for Oxford had received from Geoffrey Moore in the September 1956 issue of the *London Magazine* was fairly typical. The Australian poets, he wrote, 'seem a thoroughly nice lot of cobbers who for some reason, have decided to have a go at writing poetry'.

Nor was Australia politically or culturally of interest. The Penguin African series, begun in 1953, expanded vigorously from 1960 in support of the anti-apartheid movement. Exiled South African Ronald Segal founded and edited the radical Penguin African Library.[14] In comparison, Australia must have seemed dreary and apathetic, yearning for acceptance, and suffering from that fatal combination that had been there since 1788 – of isolation and dependence. None of the Penguin editorial staff had visited Australia, nor would other English editors for many years.

But the undercurrent Lane had perceived amongst contemporary writers and artists and his publisher's instinct for new ideas and new markets probably encouraged him to listen to the proposal to start an Australian list. There was a gentlemen's agreement that the Australian titles would be well supported by the English company with substantial orders and promotion. But Lane did not explain that the editorial

structure of the English company precluded auto-
matic acceptance of Australian books into the British
lists – as happened to the English books in Australia.
Reciprocity was not how the world worked.

The first three Australian Penguin titles, *Three
Australian Plays*, Randolph Stow's *To the Islands* and
Kangaroo Tales edited by Rosemary Wighton,
appeared in 1963, distinguished as 'Australian' by
enclosing the penguins on the covers between two
interlocked boomerangs. Someone, in a heady burst
of provincialism, had apparently approached the
Royal Melbourne Institute of Technology and persuaded them to hold a student design competition –
and the boomerangs were the result. In the 1950s
West Africa had, presumably to signal their exoti-
cism, framed their penguins in palm trees, but the
Australian colophons had the opposite effect. The
books were branded as 'not suitable for the British
market', as not real Penguins – which, in code,
meant, of course, second-rate. Patrick White's
response, on receiving advance copies of the first
titles, was to ring Geoffrey Dutton and tell him to
'Get rid of the fucking boomerangs.'[15] He was right.

The first Australian Penguins stayed in print for
many years and show what kind of gaps existed in the
market at the time. Robert Hughes, then aged
twenty-three and art critic for *Nation* and the
Observer, was signed up to write *The Art of Australia*.
Three Australian Plays contained the scripts of Alan
Seymour's *The One Day of the Year*, Hal Porter's *The
Tower* and Douglas Stewart's *Ned Kelly* – plays which

had been predictably panned by our young critics in *Theatre* magazine for not being radical enough. Geoffrey Dutton edited *The Literature of Australia* and Donald Horne was commissioned to write a book that took stock of Australia's institutions and policies and analysed contemporary attitudes.

Australia was a cultural desert, a literary *terra nullius*. Its creative voices went largely unheard except by other writers and artists, and were condemned by most academics and critics on both sides of the world. Self-loathing had been discernible since the start of the colony, and with Federation and nationhood, men like Henry Lawson and Louis Esson and, later, poet John Bray thought it their duty to warn young men of the dangers of staying in Australia. Official Historian of the First World War, C. E. W. Bean, in 1911 saw Australia as unfinished, unmade, the farms not settled. 'Australia is a big blank map, and the whole people contently sitting over it like a committee, trying to work out the best way to fill it in.'[16]

In 1964, the critics put the boots in again. It was a regular occurrence. If I hadn't been by then exposed to *Meanjin* and its writers I wouldn't have given this a moment's thought. It was what I'd grown up with, what I'd been taught. It was the natural order of things. The newspaper which broke the scandal of the new 'literary disgrace' was Rupert Murdoch's national daily, the *Australian*, launched only a few months earlier. It had declared itself 'independent' and 'free', politically progressive, advocating reforms and new standards of national reportage. We greeted it with relief and high hopes.

A few months before the publication of Donald Horne's defining book, *The Lucky Country*, Francis Hope, assistant editor of the *New Statesman and Nation*, wrote a scathing reader's report on an anthology of new Australian writing compiled at Penguin UK's request by Geoffrey Dutton. The selection included writers such as Sumner Locke Elliott, who had just won Australia's leading literary prize, the Miles Franklin, Peter Mathers, who would win it in 1966, Randolph Stow, Peter Porter, A.D. Hope, Les Murray, Judith Wright, Rosemary Dobson, Gwen Harwood, David Campbell and others. Eventually, and by sea mail whence came all editorial bad news, Hope's verdict arrived declaring the selection not worth publishing. The report, sent by the Australian editor to the contributors and leaked to the *Australian*, caused an uproar. The writing, Francis Hope had found, 'combines the vices of parochialism and an attempted superiority about parochial society; it is like a school magazine in which the school's few intellectuals parade their dislike of the school, but betray their inability to think beyond it . . . the language is tired and slack, the sort of thing that would fit very easily into a Chamber of Commerce handout . . .'[17]

The *Australian* ran indignant letters during the following week – not about Francis Hope's almost blanket dismissal of the writers (only White, Porter and Stow had been exempted) but cheering him on. The real failure was the inability of Australians 'to measure up to world standards'.

'We are in complete agreement with Francis Hope,' trumpeted two young men from the recently established, impeccably Leavisite English Department at Monash University. 'Australian writers should realize how *bad* they are. Australian literature is a history of plagiarism, dreariness and inanity . . . There is no new Australian writing worth reading. There are no Australian writers worth reading.' Another found 'Most of the names were as familiar as a packet of cornflakes and some not as appetising . . . Our writers should realize that flocking together like a gaggle of wild geese only increases their chances of being shot down.'

The Penguin editorial director in the UK who had rejected the anthology as, regrettably, of 'far too low a standard for us to publish', was Tony Godwin, a remarkable man in his own territory, responsible for considerably broadening Penguin's list from 1960–67. Dutton always suspected that, having resisted taking most titles from the new Australian list, Godwin had invited Dutton to edit an anthology of new Australian writing for a series he was commissioning from the emerging literatures in English around the world 'as a desperate act of goodwill'.

Goodwill was certainly lacking most of the time. Often the resistance came in the guise of concerns about quality management and editorial standards.

Production standards were frequently cited – and were not helped in 1966 when copies of Robert Hughes' *The Art of Australia*, hot off the Adelaide presses, were airmailed to Godwin in London and fell to pieces in his hands, confirming his prejudices about hopeless Australia.[18] Hughes naturally took advantage of the situation, insisted on major revisions and the edition was withdrawn from print and pulped. But there can be no doubt that Penguin's first editorial responses to Australian publishing were debilitating and dispiriting and Allen Lane's inability to deliver on his initial enthusiasm hard to understand. It could have come as no surprise when Brian Stonier, his Production Manager George Smith and the two 'editorial consultants' resigned together to start their own imprint, Sun Books. They had done a remarkable job of fighting for the permission and the resources to publish Australian titles. Stonier had the dual role of increasing Penguin's sales figures in Australia, while Dutton and Harris were paid modest retainers and were expected to produce books to exacting standards. And very largely they did.

Donald Horne's ironically titled *The Lucky Country* had been published late in 1964 and reluctantly supported in the UK on condition that its title was changed there to *Australia in the Sixties*. The Australian edition of the book sold 100,000 copies in its first few months. Its cover was bedecked with boomerangs and featured a splendid painting by Albert Tucker of the archetypal sun-dried Australian bloke, eyeless in the glare, mouth set tight against the flies, feather in his cap. In the top pocket of his open-necked shirt is the ace of spades but, Horne argued, his 'luck' may be just about to run out.

'Australia is a lucky country run mainly by second-rate people who share its luck,' wrote Horne. 'It lives on other people's ideas . . .'[19] Culturally it was just as bad.

> In literature and some of the arts . . . there has been all the confusion of a breakthrough . . . What over-whelms is the activity . . . Australians with cultivated tastes, or the desire to have them, largely consider theatre, music, and books as something to enjoy, to consume like a good meal: talk about it for a bit then forget it . . . But they have not developed that solemn high reverence towards Art that has been the fashion since the nineteenth century. Nor have they developed very much detailed knowledge. The result is that their reactions are spontaneous, unlearned and, very largely, ill-informed.[20]

Horne was scathing about critics, the commentators, the press, the academics, the politicians. There were far too many artists and writers for a country this size. The place was not only unsophisticated, but smug and snobbish. His reprimands were what educated Penguin readers wanted to hear in 1964 and the book reprinted steadily for many years. What strikes me now is the ferocity of the analysis given the depth of the changes that had already begun. When I first read *The Lucky Country* in 1965 on the beach on a

Greek island, I remember being quite sure that Australia was a place I had left for good.

Like thousands of other yearning young Australians in the mid-1960s, I couldn't wait to leave. Inconceivable to stay a week longer than necessary and even more inconceivable to plan to return. It was necessary to cast yourself adrift. You took only enough money to get across the seas to wherever you decided to stay. If you were a serious traveller, out of the clutches of parents and had avoided the concerns of many of your contemporaries who were starting to plan kitchen teas and choose bridesmaids, you went as soon as you could – and with no return ticket. The word was that you could earn a little money, when needed, by selling your blood to an Athens blood bank, or by teaching Australian English to migrants waiting for boats in Brindisi or Piraeus.

Many who left in the fifties and sixties did not come back, or not until things were visibly improving after Whitlam was belatedly elected in 1972. Others stayed away, made names for themselves, some by keeping up a running commentary on the cultural and literary desert they had been forced to renounce. They were often celebrated when they did return, like George Johnston and Charmian Clift, who arrived home from Hydra to find their sex lives under the microscope and their literary reputations higher than they'd dreamed. Johnston's *My Brother Jack* had won the Miles Franklin in 1964 and had immediately been hailed as a candidate for the Great Australian Novel.

The Great Australian Novel was still waiting to be written in the sixties. Many of the critics and academics of the day told us so and young men in advertising agencies dreaming up copy for Holden cars and Slazenger tennis racquets joked that they would soon be off to Greece to write it. New novels were regularly reviewed in the newspapers in the light of whether they did or did not exhibit the kind of prose style and epic sweep that fulfilled the criteria for consideration as the Great Australian Novel. There was no suggestion that a woman might produce the goods. That went without saying. The themes of race and class in novels written by women between the wars had been replaced by what the critics liked to dismiss as the small palette, the domestic, the personal – not at all the stuff of a Big Novel which would put us on the map. If Australia could produce just one great book, one that was recognized by the international literary world, that made the reading lists of universities, one that would be translated throughout Europe, that would be permanently in stock in the best bookshops of London and New York, the country could relax.

'Going to Europe,' Shirley Hazzard wrote in *The Transit of Venus*

was about as final as going to heaven. A mystical passage to another life, from which no one returned the same . . . There was nothing mythic at Sydney: momentous objects, beings, and events all occurred abroad or in the elsewhere of books. Sydney could never take for granted, as did the very meanest town in Europe, that a poet might be born there or a great painter walk beneath its windows. The likelihood did not arise, they did not feel they had deserved it. That was the measure of resentful obscurity: they could not imagine a person who might expose or exalt it.[21]

I left Australia in 1965 with a painter who was also a classical guitarist. We'd been married a few months before and spent some of the next five years pretending to other people that we weren't. He was going to Greece to paint. I was trying to write. We took with us two guitars, an Olivetti portable painted red, lots of notebooks and drawing materials and joined a ship from the British-India line which was taking Holden cars to Karachi and Kuwait and wheat to the railhead at Basrah. Peter was determined he would teach me to play Anon.'s lovely *Romance Antigua* on the long voyage around the coast of India and Pakistan and through the Persian Gulf to the Shatt-al-Arab where the Tigris and the Euphrates meet. And he did.

There were no passengers but the two of us and the Captain's Scottish wife, who lived in a British enclave in Bombay and who prided herself on walking ten miles each day around the deck of the small ship. We could hear her fast footfalls overhead as we lay on our bunk or worked at the twin polished-wood writing tables. There was no air-conditioning or swimming pool and we spent more and more time in the deep salt-water bath drinking gin and reading books as we neared the equator. We had a steward all to ourselves, a rather grand Indian, who made it clear that we were a disappointment. We failed to play bridge in the salon at night, where he opened the tiny bar whether we were there or not, and we had no guests to entertain on board in any of the ports.

The ship had a mahogany-panelled library containing a curious collection of 1950s British library fiction in glass-fronted cabinets – thrillers, romances, spy stories, travelogues – the kind of books that many Australian municipal libraries still received on standing orders. We were given a key and trusted to help ourselves. Dutifully we filled in the dark red ledger with the names and dates of the books we borrowed – and our comments for the next reader. The entries revealed the previous passengers as an idiosyncratic bunch. Some, like us, seemed merely to have taken a slow boat to Persia – eight weeks around India and the Persian Gulf, which was cheaper than flying to Europe. I imagined them reading between card games and naps, fighting the heat and boredom. '148° on deck at 5p.m.,' wrote one, 'but *The Snows of Kilimanjaro* and lots of G and Ts did the trick.'

Others, probably on their way between oil fields and jobs that were paying ten times the norm, were more demanding. '*Why no Atlas?*' was underlined furiously. 'Why no Kuwaiti dictionary?' Why indeed? The Kuwaitis by the time we got there were speaking formal English and French, the men driving

Cadillacs, their wives wearing Parisian clothes and lipstick beneath their *chadors*. We felt poor and shabby, as indeed we were.

I read my way through the Dorothy L. Sayers, and the shelves of Christie, Ngaio Marsh, and Graham Greene, as soon as it became too hot for the Olivetti. Michael Innes was a find. His *Hamlet, Revenge!*, *The Journeying Boy* and *Lament for a Maker* were memorable in ways rare in thrillers. I didn't know then that Innes was the *nom de plume* for Professor J.I.M. Stewart who, as visiting Chair of English at the University of Adelaide, from Oxford and Queen's, Belfast, had declared in 1940 that there was no Australian literature at all.

Geoffrey Dutton remembered attending the first lecture in Adelaide supported by the Commonwealth Literary Fund, given by Professor Stewart. 'I am most grateful to the C.L.F. for providing funds to give these lectures in Australian literature,' he began. 'Unfortunately they have neglected to provide any literature – I will lecture therefore on D.H. Lawrence's *Kangaroo*.'[22]

The ship's library catered for idle reading in deck chairs in the shade, not for hard information about where the Arab world was heading and taking the rest of us. There was Kipling, of course, and a few romances of the Raj that I devoured, looking for clues to the Captain and his wife, who spoke of India as if independence hadn't happened and of the Goan crew as if they were dim-witted children who preferred to sleep on deck beneath tarpaulins. As we steamed through the outbreak of hostilities between Pakistan and India – so close we could see the flash of the gunfire – British flag flying, kedgeree on the breakfast menu, curries for lunch and roast beef and Yorkshire pudding at night, it was more like being in a *Boys' Own Annual* than a serious encounter at sea.

We lived on the island of Ios in the Cyclades long enough to see all the seasons change, the tomato crop turned into dark red paste and sealed in pots and the salted fish hung in houses buttressed against the wind. The island was one of the furthest from Piraeus and had not yet made it into the guide books. There were no famous ruins or grand buildings, just white wind-mills and little churches on every headland. There were no roads, just endless steps up from the harbour and donkey tracks around the cliffs. There was a tiny square with weather-beaten tables where men sat drinking ouzo and playing cards, and a bearded priest in a high black hat who made his presence felt several times a day. There was no electricity or running water. But long after the *melteme* was freezing our fingers and toes and we'd run out of things to read around the little *petroleo* stove and the people we swapped books with had left, we stayed on playing at living the life of art on a Greek Island.

We had rented a room above the square. The vil-lagers welcomed us, then spent our rent money on refrigerators and television sets which sat in pride of place under doilies and framed photographs waiting for the day when the power supply would arrive. Every morning early Peter made his way through the ribaldry of the women to the village well with our pots and copper kettle. Later I'd climb the steps to the *yaoórti* maker who replaced yesterday's brown bowl with a fresh one full of yoghurt which had formed a creamy crust in the sun. We'd sit on the wall of the balcony eating this on new bread with honey as the village woke up. Then at opposite ends of our long narrow room with its flagstones picked out in white-wash and its peeling blue door letting in a rim of hot light, we'd work until the early afternoons.

Re-reading now what I wrote then, I find stories full of the usual clunks and awkwardnesses of first real writings, problems which I dimly perceived but had no idea how to fix. There's a piece of a novel I remember starting in a white heat of what I mistook to be inspiration, of excitement as words poured forth, as if the torrent itself meant something. What I'd been reading shows. Koestler, Camus, Durrell, Huxley, there's even an attempt at an interrogation, Rubashov style. The voice I'm using is never mine or even, I am disconcerted now to discover, female. There are no echoes of the few contemporary women writers I'd found for myself – Muriel Spark, Doris Lessing, Margaret Drabble. But I'd gone to them for information about life, I think, rather than for the kind of sacred *gravitas* I had been taught to value above all.

The voice is a first person male, an 'I' recognizable now as if from a great distance. I watch him walk, slim-hipped, of course, through narrow streets in a town somewhere on the Mediterranean. He enters a café and orders a Pernod before he leaves with a young woman in espadrilles and a swinging skirt. The 'I' is 'he' not me and not even someone I knew. He is inhabiting a place I had never been to, speaking in rhythms I do not recognize as mine. He is simply someone I have summoned to appear as Main Character in a fiction I am struggling to preside over in what reads like someone else's head.

The boat from Piraeus came once a week in winter and three times a week in summer bringing fresh fruit and a handful of visitors with paperback books in their rucksacks and bedrolls – books from Canada and California and Israel, in editions and imprints I'd never seen before. Here I first read authors who hadn't yet made it into the part of the world I'd come from.

In the long hot afternoons, after a sleep, we'd clamber down the terraced hillsides through olive trees and tomato bushes to the glittering sea. We'd read in the shade and bake ourselves on the rocks, then dive in and float with eyes wide open searching in the deep crevasses for embedded amphora and carved stones – for this, so the local stories went, was the land of Atlantis and of the goddess Isis.

Here I first read Ralph Ellison and Paul Bowles in old American paperbacks found in a secondhand bookshop in Haifa and left behind on the island by an Israeli boy called Harvey. A girl from Texas gave me Saul Bellow's *The Adventures of Augie March*, James Baldwin's *The Fire Next Time* and *The Group* by Mary McCarthy, which would be banned in Australia that year. She wrote inside the covers in large loops 'Please return to Carole', but I never did. Sometimes parcels of paperbacks would arrive from my mother at the little post office in the field below the village which opened only on the days when the boat pulled out at five o'clock in the evening. Horne's *The Lucky Country* which had been published just before we left Australia and Patrick White's *Riders in the Chariot* came in the same parcel one day, both probably selected by my mother in the hope that we would soon want to come home.

I first read *Riders in the Chariot* in the glare off the rocks on that beach in the Cyclades. It was a book that had grown out of White's sense of himself as an outcast, 'first a child with what kind of a strange gift nobody quite knew; then a despised colonial boy in an English public school; finally an artist in horrified Australia'[23] but it also emerged from post-war Australia itself, a place full of prejudice and ignorance and moments of kindness and profundity.

> Then, as people will toss up the ball of friendship, into the last light, at the moment of departure, and it will hang there briefly, lovely and luminous to see, so did the Jew and Mrs Godbold. There hung the golden sphere.

> The laughter climbed up quickly, out of their exposed
> throats, and clashed together by consent; the light splin-
> tered against their teeth. How private, and mysterious,
> and beautiful it was, even the intruders suspected, and
> were deterred momentarily from hating.[24]

Here were the big themes of the twentieth century
reverberating in ways they only could, perhaps, in
Australia, a place where there was a chance to make
something from the damaged past. A half-caste
Aboriginal painter, a mad visionary Australian spin-
ster, an intellectual Jewish refugee from the evil of the
Holocaust and a laundress who had heard Bach one
winter evening in Ely Cathedral, find themselves in
Sarsparilla, in the kind of limited world I knew and
was determined to leave behind. The craving for
experience, the impulse 'to know life' meant much
more to me than facing the uncertainties and cruelties and possibilities of the place I came from. The
imperative to escape ran deep.

Great grey London. We'd put London off for as long
as the money lasted and there were still Peter's paintings to sell in Australia and I could catch the boat
into Athens every month to the blood bank in the
narrow back street where the drachmas I was paid
covered the rent. London – the beginning and end of
so many of the stories of my childhood, where I

expected to feel at home. But of course I didn't. When I arrived, burnt dark brown from the sun, in a handmade dress, with a bag stuffed with underdone stories and notes and a blue and white *flokati* woven as a farewell present by Irene, our Ios landlady, I was foreign and knew it at once.

A week later Greece was a mirage. I'd walked into a job in the Publications Branch of the British Council in High Holborn where I catalogued onto cards British books I never saw for exhibitions in Nairobi and Johannesburg and on to Sydney. Peter was accepted by the Inner London Education Authority for a position teaching art to West Indian children in Brixton whose only playground was a huge wire cage on the school roof.

We queued and miraculously were selected to rent an ancient top-floor studio flat in a building which backed on to the District and Circle lines at South Kensington but which fronted on to Thurloe Square opposite the Victoria and Albert Museum. We had a key to the garden and could watch the rich gently exercising old English sheepdogs and basset hounds in the evening and nannies guarding small children during the day. The studio had been built to house artists attached somehow to the V&A and I imagined art classes with models reclining against draped velvet bathed in the gentle northern light that flooded in through the huge skylight. Lying in bed on the mezzanine we built, we could watch clouds scudding overhead and once, in October, we saw the swallows wheel and head south.

Life, as it always does, intervened without me trying. London rapidly became no more than the city where I happened to live, where I went to the library and the pub each week and queued for the laundrette and cheap theatre tickets, where I caught the underground in the dark on winter mornings and walked home through Hyde Park from Marble Arch in summer. A few blocks away in Knightsbridge and Chelsea swinging London was wearing mini skirts and Vidal Sassoon haircuts and sipping bad coffee out of Union Jack mugs and I too shopped at Biba in Kensington High Street and Habitat in the Kings Road, the Stones and the Beatles always in the air.

London was where my daughter was born. I spent the afternoons in the months before her birth, and many afterwards with her in a sling, walking the endless rooms of the Victoria and Albert Museum across the square in the Cromwell Road. At first its enormous and eccentric collection of the 'world's applied art' seemed utterly random to me, but slowly I began to make some kind of sense of the plastercasts and electrotypes of Baptistery doors and Gothic portals, the rood screens and tall stone crosses. Nativity terracottas and ivories and alabasters from mediaeval England and Italy flowed seamlessly into the vast collections of Islamic, Indian and Chinese art assembled with the unerring eye and confident aesthetic of English collectors of a certain class and era.

Of course I did not ponder the lack in the collection of any applied Australian art. It went without saying that there wasn't any deemed suitable to be included. Not even an emu egg surrounded by silver filigreed Aborigines or a colonial governor's secretaire of Huon pine or a christening robe intricately embroidered for a squatter's child by a convict servant-girl. Next door in the Natural History Museum the Tasmanian devil and the platypus had made the grade, and the three and a half ton 'Cranbourne meteor from Australia' drew crowds of schoolchildren.

I only half remember how the decision to return home after nearly three years away was taken, certainly it would have been lightly, as those decisions seem to be. A craving for sunshine after a bad winter, certainly. An advertisement on the underground for cheap fares, quite likely. And, yes, a need to be part of the changes and the political unrest we were hearing about from friends, as if from the bottom of a well, and sometimes tucked away in the London papers – news about Australia's commitment of troops to support America's efforts in Vietnam.

But in any case I knew in my bones that it was inconceivable that my daughter, and in little more than a year my son, should grow up anywhere else.

3

Something to Do
During the Day

'Your application is most timely,' wrote John Michie, then General Manager of Penguin Books Australia, in his letter asking me to come for an interview for the new job of Editorial Assistant, in early 1969. And, as things turned out, it was.

First, I'd contacted the universities to try to return to Australian Prehistory, but there was no one to supervise a thesis based on fieldwork unless I could get myself to the Australian National University in Canberra, where John Mulvaney was establishing the School of Pacific Studies. Editing and young children seemed likely to be more manageable. There wasn't a lot of choice. My contemporaries were mainly nurses, physiotherapists, schoolteachers and wives. The Australian Broadcasting Commission and the daily papers offered cadetships, mainly to men. I was struggling in secret to write a sentence I was pleased with.

Editing, I thought, meant a desk in a quiet room

with shelves full of reference books and manuscripts piled high waiting to be turned mysteriously into books; and it looked a little more interesting than the other roles available at the time to middle-class girls with arts degrees who liked reading. So, grossly exaggerating my experience in London and concealing somehow the fact that I had little idea what it was that publishers did, I had written to Penguin when I decided to return to work. All I knew was that Penguin published most of the books that had shaped my reading life and that of my family and friends.

Penguin was also only half an hour's drive down the winding mountain road in our old VW. We had returned to Australia to build a studio and a writing room amongst the tree ferns on eight acres of cheap hillside high up on the south-eastern slopes of the Dandenongs. On a fine day you could see the sea, and on a winter's morning the fog blanketing the mountain came only up to the front gate at the end of the unmade track we intended to turn into a sweeping drive one day.

For much of the year it was a quagmire and in summer there was often the smell of smoke and fire alarms in the middle of the night when bushfires threatened. But it was cool and beautiful and there were remnants of a garden with blue hydrangeas and rhododendrons grown wild up the slope behind the pair of one-room wooden cabins that were only just standing when we found them. Their previous life had probably been as part of a 1920s boarding house linked by walkways to a central dining-room and kitchen. There was no running water so we sank a well beside a spring and my first pay cheque would go towards the ten light poles we had to provide before the electricity could be brought up from the road.

We had it all worked out. Peter would build a studio from mudbricks made on the place, then paint his pictures and teach part-time at a local technical school. I would bake bread in the old slow combustion stove, grow vegetables on the slope behind the house and have a year or two working full-time. When neither of us could be at home the children would be cared for by another mother nearby. Then, when the studio and a room for me were built according to the plans pinned up in the kitchen, we'd both stay home and paint and write. How sure we were and how simple it sounds.

Penguin Australia turned out to be housed in a suite of what looked to me extremely modern and glamorous offices outside Ringwood with a view towards the same mountains, about an hour coming the other way from the city through Melbourne's interminable eastern suburbs until the market gardens ran out and the bush began. The building had been designed by Brian Lewis, Professor of Architecture at Melbourne University. The warehouse, a fraction of its present size, seemed vast and was built on one side of a central courtyard. Everywhere was the work of Australian artists. On the front of the building hung a Robert Klippel, there was a fountain and a sculpture by Ian Bow in the courtyard – and my first sight of John Michie, in a blue denim shirt that matched his eyes, was of him sitting in front of Albert Tucker's painting of the archetypal Australian that I'd first seen on Ios on the cover of *The Lucky Country*.

I don't remember being interviewed. Instead there was a slightly surprising conversation about our children and Greece and sailing and the kind of publishing Penguin could do in Australia. Then I was shown the computer and the pulp bin in the warehouse where books damaged in transit or misbound by the printer were flung, and invited to help myself. By then I wanted the job badly – and it seemed that I had got it.

In 1969, the Australian company was doing well and they were fully aware of the fact. Just the month before I arrived, Penguin Australia had noted in its Board papers that 'It was resolved to grant a loan to the parent company in the UK of $200,000 at 7 per cent interest per annum.' The English company was not thriving at the end of the sixties and this was the first of many such loans.[1] The end-of-month sales figures, the better-than-forecast return on investment, were celebrated in the office before they were reported triumphantly to Harmondsworth in the UK.

As something to do during the day, publishing is about as good as it gets, John would say. There were about twenty-five office staff, a sales force and a warehouse worked mainly by women recently arrived from the north of England. The management group, young men in their twenties and early thirties, graduates, were impatient to expand the company and publish more Australian books. There were books waiting to be commissioned about the shift in the social and political climate. There was much talk of re-shaping the publishing map of the world, as if it made every sense to make Penguin Australia the hub of southern hemisphere publishing and distribution. Books could then be shipped into Japan, Singapore, India, Hong Kong, Indonesia and the Philippines much more efficiently from Australia – rather than supplied by slow boat out of London. Books about the region were already under way but they would not be read anywhere but in Australia. This seemed even then like talking to ourselves and opportunities lost. *The Poms are half asleep. We are running rings around them. They have no idea how the world works.*

That's how they all talked.

I spent my first fortnight in the warehouse learning to source books by the numbers on their spines and packing them so they would arrive at the other end in mint condition. There was a brand-new conveyor belt and visitors were shown proudly the boxes of orders chugging the length of the warehouse to the trucks in the loading bay. My feet were swollen by morning tea as each day I went backwards and forwards on the concrete floor plucking books to fill orders. But I was starry-eyed. My lunch hours were spent sitting on the rim of the pulp bin salvaging and reading books. My bookshelves are still skewed by them: Pelican histories of ancient times and places, collections of young British poets I'd never heard of and never would again, guides to English counties and great cathedrals.

Most of the early Penguins were still in print and were arranged on pallets and on open shelves by number. Here, it seemed, laid out before me, was the physical reality of the world's literature in English. I knew nothing about copyright zones or publishers as filters and only enough about contemporary American literature to recognize that most of the American titles available in Penguins then were those that had been around long enough to become Modern Classics – Henry James, Nathaniel Hawthorne. Some twentieth-century writers were there – Faulkner, Updike, Wilder, Hemingway, Steinbeck, Mailer, Miller, whose *The Colossus of Maroussi* was part of the reason some of us had gone to Greece – but younger writers and American women mostly had to wait until the seventies.

Martin Boyd's *Lucinda Brayford* had been the first Australian writer to be included in Penguin's list in 1951. Patrick White's *The Tree of Man*, published in Penguin in 1961, was followed by Alan Moorehead's *No Room in the Ark* in 1962 and *The White Nile* in 1963. The rest of White's titles followed during the sixties. But Arthur Upfield, an Englishman who'd come to live in Australia in 1911, was by far the most prolific. He had two books in Penguin in the early fifties then a further six in the 1960s. With titles like

Murder Down Under and *The Widows of Broome*, they
starred half-caste detective Napoleon Bonaparte,
who had almost magical powers and uttered some
memorable lines. 'As the mind of the Occidental differs widely from that of the Oriental, so differs as
widely the minds of the Australian black tracker and
the Australian white policeman. My birth and training fashion me into a bridge spanning the gulf
between them.'[2] Upfield's outback settings, such as
Broome where 'the majority of people walked with
somnambulistic tread and day-dreamed of the glorious past when booze was cheap'[3], appealed to English
and Australian readers alike.

There were twenty-seven Australian Penguins by
early 1969. No Australian books were regarded as
Modern Classics. Henry Handel Richardson hadn't
yet made it, nor Stead, nor Miles Franklin. Eleanor
Dark would have to wait for Virago.

Everything the company did was considered useful
background for an editor. The number of outlets for
books were expanding around Australia and, as this
was a time of building new universities to cater for
massive increases in student numbers, sales by
Penguin into the new courses and departments of
anthropology, sociology, psychology and environmental and behavioural sciences were providing a
large part of their new growth. There was a small and
enthusiastic sales force who often came up with ideas
for books that were needed. There was even a commission agent who worked the South Pacific and
Papua New Guinea and who belonged to an earlier

era. Colonel Penfold arrived twice a year in a light safari suit and nautical-looking shoes. He'd replenish his supplies of paperbacks from a small selection of titles, pack them in large suitcases alongside the pens and paper he also sold, tell a few swashbuckling traders' stories and depart for the islands.

Ordering from the offices in Ringwood to the warehouse in Harmondsworth had become an art-form. Stockholdings were meticulously noted on the company drum file by the operations manager in a small office that was a kind of nerve centre of the company.

But across the corridor the future had already arrived. Here was the state-of-the-art computer, a massive drum-drive and printers, programmed by an imperturbable young woman called Irene Vale. The computer took up a whole office on one side of the courtyard which had its own special air-conditioning plant installed. It ruled until disk-drives arrived a few years later and enabled the warehouse to be linked daily to the stock control system.

The manual system ran in tandem with the computer for the first few months after I arrived. The operations manager, John Powers, correctly predicted that the computer would break down, but his colleagues suspected a deep reluctance to part with his perfect process, the superior virtues of which were extolled at length to his captive trainee editor who was set to add the day's data to each card, in pencil in case I got it wrong. The drum file was a large metal bin on casters which was padlocked at the end of the

day. Inside was a card system that mapped the move-
ments of every title Penguin had ever published –
every educational setting, every special sale, every
delay on the docks, every reprint in the pipeline.
Here was the physical reality of shipping books across
the world, into a warehouse in Victoria and out again
to bookshops all over the country. Eventually Powers
was taken to a long lunch at the Bird and Bottle
while his drum file was trundled from his office to
the back of the warehouse and from there, no doubt,
to the local tip. Someone should have thought to save
it. But the impulse for change in workplaces then as
now was at odds with any archival consciousness.

Where the books were placed in the monthly publications list was, at the time, highly political. Pressure
might sometimes come from Harmondsworth to
feature a title they had overstocks of, or that was a
bestseller in the UK but of only minor interest in
Australia. Even if it was obvious that sales of the few
new Australian publications were likely to exceed the
English titles that month, the decision to place them
on the front of the monthly order sheet had to
be negotiated with the UK. Decisions were monitored, sales were reported – and copies sent to
Harmondsworth each month. It was a long time before
there was a recognition that the two markets were
already very different and likely to become more so.

My induction month included a week in a bookshop – at Robertson & Mullens where so many of my
grandmother's books had come from. I was put in the
charge of John Burchall's staff – unpacking Penguins,

monitoring stock, serving customers and starting to understand how the company was seen in the retail trade. I went out with the sales representatives to the new Monash University campus bookshop in Clayton, to the dauntingly superior Hill of Content bookshop where Michael Zifcak presided and to several suburban stores in the new shopping centres.

By the time I returned to my small office with its desk against the window and the sounds of bellbirds from the creek, I had some idea what publishing books involved. Now I had to work out what part editors played. I knew I had to deal with printers, designers, authors, other publishers and satisfy the requirements of Harmondsworth, which expected to see copies of covers and finished books before publication. I spent weeks with the files trying to work out the system.

One of the great strengths of Penguin worldwide in those years was its meticulous attention to design and production detail. Hans Schmoller, and before him, Jan Tschichold, had set the standards of what was called, even in Australia, 'Penguin livery'. Tschichold, trained first in Switzerland and then Germany, had joined Penguin as Art Director in 1947, bringing a coherence that had been eroded during the war when Penguin's list had grown rapidly. His was a traditionalism which believed that good design and typography should not be obvious. His covers incorporated asymmetry, sanserif typefaces, photographic illustration and primary colours – probably the start of what had so offended my grandmother. It was

Tschichold who initiated Penguin's *Composition Rules* which were given to every new editor and designer throughout the Penguin Group. Regularly revised, they allowed his stamp to be on every book – and the books to be models of standardization and consistency within strict typographical principles. Many titles were set in Stanley Morison's Times New Roman of 1931: '. . . they evoked something fresh and modern while not being so rarefied or "moderne" as to discourage the customer from picking them up'.[4]

The most detailed instructions for production managers in Penguin companies worldwide related to the use of the Penguin colophon itself. It must face into the page, to the left on the spine, to the right on the back. Its size was determined by design criteria established by Tschichold and Schmoller, and the Australian company, and no doubt Penguin West Africa and Penguin Canada as well, was swiftly reprimanded if they got it wrong.

My copy of Randolph Stow's *To the Islands*, Penguin, 1963, numbered AU1, the huge Penguin colophon on the front cover looking rather startled to find itself between towering boomerangs, I found in the pulp bin. It is sewn into its spine and still opens well. The typesetting is impeccable but the margins are all over the place. Stow's *The Merry-Go-Round in the Sea* published in Penguins five years later must have given Hans Schmoller apoplexy. The spine cracks at every page-opening, the glue is visible, the book feels like a block and the typesetting is gappy and uneven. As Schmoller kept sternly reminding the

Australian company, 'Close word-spacing is one of the basic rules of good composition and your printer evidently does not know it.'[5]

When books arrived in the warehouse from Australian printers, I was instructed by John Michie how to test them by grasping a page from the middle of the book, holding it at arm's length and flicking it as hard as you could. This was an agonizing moment. If the glue held and the pages didn't flutter to the floor, the stock was accepted. Books with spines sealed in 'hot melt' glue, which suited English conditions, had a habit, after crossing the Nullarbor in a heatwave, of arriving in Perth in pieces. 'Cold melt' on the other hand could fall apart in the northern hemisphere, which was probably what had happened to Robert Hughes' first print run. Glues had been a source of tension for years, I was told.

Book-quality paper was scarce, too. It often gave way when it was flicked, it yellowed rapidly and its grain was a problem. There was still a letter on the file from Hans Schmoller to Brian Stonier, 'One thing that is wrong with your paper is the direction of the grain: it runs across the page instead of down. It is this which prevents the book from lying flat when opened, and if you ever order a whole making, you should try to insist that the paper is supplied with the grain running parallel with the spine on the finished book.'[6] Australian printers, unless guaranteed a steady flow of orders, were reluctant to upgrade their plant and change their ways.

Australian post-war book design until the late

sixties was almost non-existent. A few art schools taught graphic design and the principles of typography with advertising in mind but printers and publishers rarely employed the services of typographers or designers. It was common practice to leave layout to printers or to give them a sample page torn from an English book of vaguely similar content with the instruction to 'follow style'. And they did as best they could. Since the vast majority of books sold in Australia were imported, few printers had been able to specialise in book production. Most manufactured cardboard cartons or printed a range of directories as well. The availability of typefaces was limited. Letter spacing, where the type is finely tuned with hairspaces, was almost unknown.

A number of books were waiting for me when I arrived, at various stages of readiness for the printer. Most had been previously published in hardcovers, and were in the process of being 'taken over' by John Michie, their paperback rights acquired from their hardback publishers. This meant that no editing was required for books such as Barry Oakley's *A Wild Ass of a Man*, *The Letters of Rachel Henning*, Thomas Keneally's *Three Cheers for the Paraclete*. If their margin widths and type sizes were good enough for Penguin, their pages could be photographically reduced for paperback. If not, they had to be re-set and proofed.

My job was to prepare the books according to grids and guidelines laid down at Harmondsworth, to gradually upgrade all the old Australian covers and to write new cover blurbs.

The covers were dreary, often black and white pen drawings picked out in 'Penguin orange' and they were still all carrying the Australian colophon with its boomerangs, like 1950s tea towels. I searched the files but could find no guidelines covering boomerangs and one of my first editorial acts was to suggest to the General Manager that we do away with the boomerangs. And we did – and curiously gratifying I found it was even then.

Before I arrived, John Michie had been trying to persuade the Penguin editors to take copies of Henry Handel Richardson's *The Fortunes of Richard Mahony*, continuing the arguments first had by Stonier, Dutton and Harris. I spent many hours seeking perfect paintings for the jackets of the three volumes and trying to imagine what might illuminate the novel for British readers as well as our own, just in case the Penguin editors relented and ordered a few. I commissioned and gingerly copy-edited a scholarly introduction from Leonie Kramer, then Professor of Australian Literature at Sydney University, for whom Richard Mahony was 'the first substantial character in Australian fiction'. Despite the absence of boomerangs and my beautiful covers featuring paintings by Arthur Streeton and Tom Roberts, the English editors once again turned the trilogy down. Having been first published in England by William Heinemann in three volumes between 1917 and 1929, *The Fortunes of Richard Mahony* was listed in the British stocklist as 'Australian edition only'.

Thomas Keneally's *Bring Larks and Heroes* and *Three Cheers for the Paraclete* had been published by Angus & Robertson a few years earlier. They were planning their own paperback imprint and were reluctant to let any of their classic backlist go to Penguin. But their editor, John Abernethy, a good friend of John Michie, and soon of mine, was someone who was enthusiastic about Penguin Australia's ambitions to build a list and agreed to make a number of recent titles available. Re-settings were usually necessary and, desperate for guidance and basic typographical skills, I was taken under the wing of Arthur Stokes, who was then in charge of the Melbourne office of Halstead Press, a printery. Arthur, one of the few classically trained typographers in the country, would, if asked, stop being a printer for a while and explain to me with meticulous pencilled diagrams the fundamentals of typefaces and letter-spacing. His advice I combined with Penguin's *Composition Rules*, and managed to fudge my way through my first year, learning on the run.

Midway through 1969, John Hooker, who had been publishing for some time at F.W. Cheshire, was appointed as senior editor with a brief to expand the Australian list. He was to do this by commissioning titles for an original paperback list that reflected the changes that had been happening in Australia since the mid-1960s. Whitlam's government with its

progressive agenda was still a couple of years off – but
Penguin, with a staff who were ambitious to restart
its publishing programme, was beginning to commission titles reflecting the times. There was a demand
for books that analysed our national character and
changing sense of ourselves, which neatly dovetailed
with the hunger that Penguin had been catering for
all over the English-speaking world for literature in
affordable editions.

The Vietnam War had divided the nation, environmental concerns had been thrown into sharp
relief with the mining boom that had made the place
feel like the world's quarry, women's liberation was
beginning to be heard in the distance, and educational and social welfare issues were being
vehemently debated. In 1967 Australians had voted
overwhelmingly to give full citizenship to Aboriginal
people and there was optimism in the air about what
that would mean. In the arts, too, what had begun in
the early sixties was escalating and would soon seem
like a great awakening – in music, in painting, in an
Australian film industry that was about to re-emerge.
At La Mama and the Australian Performing Group in
Carlton, which had grown out of the student theatre
of a few years before, and at the Nimrod in Sydney
some of the most radical and innovative theatre in the
country could be seen. And one of the first original
Australian Penguins I put together was a volume of
plays from the Australian Performing Group. *Plays*,
published in 1970 with an introduction by Graeme
Blundell, contained Alexander Buzo's *The Front*

Room Boys, Jack Hibberd's *Who?* and *White with Wire Wheels*, and John Romeril's *Chicago, Chicago*.

When original manuscripts started arriving – Richard Harding's *Police Killings in Australia*, and Humphrey McQueen's *A New Britannia* – I began to edit in the sense of working with authors to help restructure and fine-tune new work. Both books were examples of the new radicalism, of the social change that had been gaining momentum with each election.

But even in a company as modern as Penguin, there was still a strong sense from the directors and staff in London that Australia was an outpost, that the Australian company was really a branch office and must be told what was best for it and for the Australian market. The fledgling Australian publishing programme, it was made clear, was a reward for selling British books well. This attitude was expressed in different ways – in letters not replied to, in cables received announcing decisions but giving no reasons, in phone calls at 3a.m. asking for funds to be transmitted, presumably at the end of a long London day: sales down, scotch in hand and our man in Australia on the line.

The majority of publishing companies in Australia were branch offices of British publishers in every sense of the term. When the Chairman of a major London-based publishing house declared at a British booksellers' dinner that all he needed in Australia was a 'chimp with a crowbar to open the crates' he was only half joking. Warehousing and distribution of books could be done by Australians with organizational skills and market know-how, people who could add up and remit a satisfactory return to the parent company every quarter. The last thing that was wanted was a graduate in literature or history to manage a company's subsidiary. Mention was made in UK Board minutes of the private schools and hobbies of Australian general managers. Sailing or wine-growing reassured members that the fellow out there was a 'chap'. General managers were chosen because they could protect the company's investment in Australia. If they could turn on a good Melbourne Cup Week and get members' tickets for the Test, so much the better.

British chairmen and export directors visited regularly and were received by their local companies with a mixture of deference and straight-talking which could turn to jokes and mimicry as soon as they departed. The Australian book trade delighted in stories of stilted small talk at backyard barbecues, fatally formal dressing and jetlagged British bosses falling asleep in their lobster thermidor.

I could see what John and the others were talking about – that publishers were instrumental in what was available for reading. That the long wait for orders to arrive by sea, the shortage in Australia of contemporary writing by Americans, Canadians, South Africans, New Zealanders and Australians was the direct result of the Territorial Copyright Agreement which carved the world up into copyright zones. The main English language markets were crudely and anachronistically divided into two – North America and its territories and Britain and its traditional export markets stemming from Empire, and including Australia and New Zealand. Books first published in the States, but not acquired by British publishers, rarely came into Australia. And there were many of them. The books we read in Australia were largely the result of decisions taken somewhere else.

At the end of the sixties, Australia was changing fast but it still had farcical censorship laws in place. Imported books could be challenged under Federal legislation and also state by state. The Federal laws on importation were rigid enough but even books deemed suitable for public consumption by the Federal Government could still be banned by one or all of the states, as had happened when Mary McCarthy's *The Group* was banned in Victoria in 1966 or when *Lady Chatterley's Lover* was allowed in by South Australian Premier Don Dunstan in the mid-sixties, but its sale forbidden by Victorian Premier Henry Bolte. Then *The Trial of Lady Chatterley*, the published account of the British legal challenge mounted by Allen Lane and Penguin Books in 1961, which quoted extensively from the novel, was banned throughout Australia. Only when copies were printed in Australia by Penguin in support of a legal challenge by the

Council of Civil Liberties was it quietly released. By printing in Australia rather than importing the book the company was not technically subject to Federal censorship laws although it could still be prosecuted state by state.

In 1970, when over ninety titles remained on the banned list, including many works of literature such as Nabokov's *Lolita,* Hubert Selby Jnr's *Last Exit to Brooklyn*, Henry Miller's *The Tropic of Cancer,* William S. Burroughs' *Naked Lunch*, John Michie decided that Penguin was in a strong enough position to again challenge the legislation. 'The effect of this policy,' he wrote in the *Bulletin*, 'has been to turn Australia into the Alabama of the literary world . . . and Australia's position relative to most countries is now somewhat further behind than at any other stage in its history.'[7]

Portnoy's Complaint by Philip Roth had been published in the States and by Jonathan Cape in the UK in 1969, when Michie and Hooker made an offer for the Australian paperback rights. Corgi had acquired them but were unwilling to risk publishing in Australia; instead they accepted a sub-rights deal for the then huge sum of $10,000. Copies of the Cape edition were smuggled in for offsetting. Adelaide printers Griffin Press pulled out at the last minute, ironically on the advice of the less conservative Dunstan Government's Attorney-General, and the smaller Halstead Press in Sydney, owned by Angus & Robertson, offered to print the book. Within eighteen days of the order being placed, 75,000 copies were printed and delivered around the country to booksellers Penguin had agreed to indemnify.

On 18 August 1970, *Portnoy's Complaint* was published in Australia. The massive clandestine distribution, only possible with Penguin's computerised invoicing and despatch system, worked like a military operation and by the time the police arrived queues had formed in bookshops around the country as the book went on sale, but the only two copies in the Penguin offices were the two John Michie had waiting on his desk. It was heady stuff. Things would never be the same again and we all knew it. And the book, a satirical monologue of a tormented adolescent challenging the constraints of the older generation, was just the one to start to bring down the old censorship system.

John Michie, John Hooker and Finance Director Peter Froelich were charged with making available an obscene publication and would spend many months in and out of court in cases which dragged on for years. There was no shortage of formidable witnesses prepared to speak in Penguin's defence. Patrick White, in an austere black coat and a homburg, looking for all the world like a British banker, testified in his great rolling voice that the book was 'a minor classic among comic novels . . . with tragic overtones' and that the offensive words *cunt*, *prick*, *fuck* were 'the kind of words that man would say'. Queen's Counsel Peter Brusey, retained by a publishing company committed to the idea of unrestricted access to whatever the public wanted to read, and people prepared to stand up and challenge the concept of *community standards*, had won the day.

Those two years at Penguin changed my life and a lot of other people's as well. John Michie and I eventually and painfully left our marriages and began to live together – incurring the disapproval of the parent company, some of our colleagues and a few of our friends. *Truth* newspaper, during the first *Portnoy* hearing, staked out our house trying to photograph us and get a scandal piece – Michie, peddler of pornography, living in sin with his editor and her two small children. The Australian and UK Boards were formally notified of my existence and I was politely given to understand that I could never have a pay rise or a promotion again. John Hooker, by then a friend but, of course, also an ambitious colleague, took his boss out to lunch and protested that he couldn't be expected to work with 'a mate's mistress' who might know more than he did sometimes about what was going on. The three of us then had a drink and agreed it was very hard on Hooker.

It was hard on me too – but it didn't occur to me to protest, and in any case I was in love. I'd bundled the children, the dog and a high chair into the car one day and had driven down the mountain into my new life. As long as I was happy, I thought, the children would be fine. The extended family had been invented by 1969. Jealousy was outlawed. So was remorse. Everyone, surely, would behave well. I thought it would all be plain sailing.

I rented a house in Mont Albert where John came to live with me and I'd rush home to play company hostess to visiting British directors. There was a changing of the guard at Penguin UK after Allen Lane's death in 1970, Pearson acquired the company and the new hierarchy visited its successful subsidiary often. Chairman Jim Rose, Christopher Dolley, Peter Calvocoressi and Ron Blass would pretend with great dignity that they hadn't met me and discussed new books in the office during the day. I'd light the candles and pass off Fray Bentos steak-and-kidney pies as my own and the next morning would be sent flowers like the good company wife I was after hours.

But I was getting up three hours earlier than anyone else in the house, driving the children to pre-school on the other side of the city and getting to work on time. We called it 'keeping the show on the road'.

The Female Eunuch was published just a few months after I allowed myself to be despatched to a firm of management consultants who were looking for someone to edit their reports. I went quietly away branded with my scarlet letter, telling nobody about the tears shed in the carpark. My precious job was in ruins but already I had begun to have a faint idea of what was possible if ideas drove a company and the management skills were there to create not only an efficient distribution machine, but the conditions where a group of people could work together to make things happen.

But first I had to have a spell in the wilderness. The old boys' network swung into action and McKinsey agreed to take me on. They had only recently arrived on the Australian scene but were well established around the world. Its consultants were Harvard Business School trained and young, several of them my contemporaries from Melbourne University. This was the first era of consultant-as-guru, called in to restructure and modernize Australian industry and banking during the years of the mining boom and rapid economic growth. Their systems were impeccable. Their language well-modulated MBA – public school with a Harvard overlay. Their reports were drafted and redrafted until their maxims gleamed and their analysis and recommendations were irrefutable.

The view from their Collins Street offices was the best I'd ever seen. From there I saw the West Gate Bridge fall down. And there I discovered I was good at spotting hot air and rectifying managerial language. There, after a few months, I was paid the ultimate compliment of being invited to train as 'the first woman consultant on our team', but was warned that clients would be asked if they objected to having a woman along – and most of them probably would, the senior consultant warned me.

Then one weekend, in mid-1971, I was sent home with instructions to prepare a briefing note on 'the government's recent achievements in tertiary and secondary education' as the basis for a draft policy paper for the Liberal Party. I tried but could think of nothing. Nor could John. I went in on Monday, resigned and then, good embryonic radical feminist that I was, backgrounded a mate on the *Australian* who, like everyone else I knew, was predicting a change of government as not only unavoidable but long overdue.

Another job was invented for me, or rather was invented to help out John, I suspect, and John Burchall came to my rescue. Again I was to be the first editorial staff appointment, this time at William Heinemann where Burchall now was, in Inkerman Street, St Kilda, a tiny subsidiary of a long established and highly regarded British publishing house. After the glories of the Penguin offices opening on to the courtyard, the fountain and the state-of-the-art computer, Heinemann was a shock. Housed in a hideous brown brick box up on stilts above a loading bay and carpark, without a bird or a leaf in sight, the company was a classic of the era established with distribution and record-keeping in mind. The staff were slightly eccentric, bookish and devoted to maverick Burchall, a spectacular long-luncher, and a great reader who had been a dedicated city bookseller for many years. Like many other companies at the time, Heinemann got by with a literary consultant on its books who occasionally recommended local titles for publication and was produced to help talk to visiting British authors at lunch. Heinemann retained literary magazine *Overland*'s editor, Stephen Murray-Smith – but no editorial staff at all.

Now Burchall had some publishing lined up for me – the company had published only spasmodically in the past. My book contracts had to be countersigned in London and contained a clause allowing for the payment of colonial royalties. This time I was to edit, design, and supervise the printing of about fifteen hardcover books a year and reject what seemed like hundreds of others. I was thrown in the deep end once more.

Several manuscripts were waiting – and had been there for a while. The largest and most intimidating was a great story of discovery and interpretation. Keast Burke, an elderly photographic historian, had unearthed in 1952 over 600 *carte-de-visite* glass plates which had turned out to be scenes of the small NSW mining towns of Hill End and Gulgong taken by travelling photographers Beaufoy Merlin and Charles Bayliss in 1872. The goldfields photographs had been commissioned by wealthy gold-miner, Bernard Otto Holtermann, and preserved in negative form.

The coverage of the towns was almost complete. There were the main streets, shop by shop, with their wooden verandahs and elaborately painted signs announcing the circulating library, the hotels, the tobacconist, the telegraph office and the undertaker. There were the mines with their batteries and shafts and miners at work in the mud. And outside the tents and cottages, the slab huts and boarding houses, the women and children posed in their best clothes.

Keast Burke and his wife Iris had worked for many years to enlarge the prints from the glass plate negatives to reveal their astonishing detail and then painstakingly to identify the faces and events in the towns. The manuscript was in that state so familiar to experienced editors, new to me, of massive overload of detail. There were hundreds of captions and notes to the captions, all displaying their erudition and local knowledge and the author's inability to let go of any element of a pioneering project that had consumed so much of his life. It was my first illustrated book – and it sat on my desk in a huge carton, prints and details from every photograph, many thousands of words of text full of inconsistencies and endless corrections in wavering handwriting. There were poems by Iris Burke and endorsements by elderly contributors to the *Australian Photo-Review*, of which Keast Burke had been the editor from 1922–56. And it came with an editor's nightmare attached – a demanding and knowledgeable author made understandably irritable by having heard nothing for some time from a publisher who had accepted the book with alacrity – then, I expect, found it all too hard.

Inevitably, I was cast by the author and his wife as

the enemy. My inexperience undoubtedly showed. Every suggestion for organising the material was rejected; the several prefaces, every caption, every poem, were essential. Each photograph had to be reproduced, they both insisted, in full as well as in detail. David Wire, a graphic designer who had trained at the Royal College of Art in London and whom I'd first met in Greece, came to my rescue. He knew about type and fine printing. Duotones were essential, Keast Burke insisted, which my reference books told me was an expensive process for reproducing photographs in several tones – in this case the finest gradations of sepias. We worked night and day to produce a beautiful book that did the collection justice. The editing and design took a year. The author and I never met. Mrs Burke answered my phone calls. We exchanged letters – mine gradually becoming firmer as I felt more sure of my ground and the costs mounted – until the dreadful day when Iris Burke rang John Burchall to report that her husband had collapsed while reading one of my letters.

Gold and Silver was published in a slip cover for something like the astronomical price of $35 a copy and later had a long life as a paperback. The author kept his silence with me, but John Burchall was eventually profusely thanked. The slides, preserved now in the Holtermann Collection in Sydney's Mitchell Library, form one of the best known historical photographic collections in the country.

It was a book that took me not only inside the most difficult of editing and production processes,

but also inside the lives of the people in the photographs. I became almost as familiar with their faces as
Keast Burke must have been and I never forgot them.
Mrs Sam Hand and her prosperous Chinese husband
and child pose outside the slab hut which was their
boarding house; the men in the butcher's shop standing
astride stare back at us, great sides of beef hanging overhead; the pregnant girl-child with the desperate face
holding her wedding ring. These *cartes* would have
been sent in letters to Cornwall and Devon, to
London's East End, to China, all over Europe to reassure families and persuade friends that the Australian
colonies in this time of gold were indeed places of
opportunity. The touches of handmade lace and a gera-
nium in a pot in the window of a wooden shack with
a bark roof, its carefully carved shutters contrasting
with the bleak huts of the miners without women –
the details would have been pondered over and passed
from hand to hand.

John Burchall became a great friend and advocate
during the two years I was with Heinemann. He
knew the secondhand book market, and collected
editions of rare Australiana and recordings of great
singers, which he'd play to us late at night. I first
heard Galli-Curci and Dame Clara Butt singing
'Land of Hope and Glory' in Hyde Park in the
Burchall sitting-room at 2 a.m. – over and over
again. John drank prodigious amounts of red wine
and rarely ate – but his intelligence and his courtesy
never deserted him.

He backed me to the hilt when I started to have

ideas of my own for books we could commission. One of these came from scriptwriter Fred Parsons who brought me photographs, scripts and the beginnings of a biography of Roy Rene, whose material he had written for many years. Rene's Mo McCackie of McCackie Mansions had brought the house down on radio and in the theatre between 1935-54. Roy Rene, in the great tradition of Jewish comedians, had blasted his way through to the core of Australian anti-Semitism and stereotyping by embodying it in the character Mo McCackie, a bisexual music hall Jew, performed in whiteface with a black beard and hooked nose.

When, in 1973, Patricia Edgar at LaTrobe University invited me to co-author *Media She*, a book on how women were treated by the media, the company promoted it widely. 'The chief stooge of the media man is woman,' the blurb declared. 'She is the sweet and simple feminine stereotype who "lightens" the pages of even our most responsible newspapers, whose body and smile sell us anything from tractor tyres to stramit ceilings, who gazes down at us from hoardings, and flits across our screens, whose imagined sexuality is laughed at, yet lusted for.'[8]

Two male students with beards and long hair agreed to be photographed in cheesecake role reversals with captions such as 'Peek-a-boo boys, it's spring', and 'She never came home for dinner on time until I discovered Hair-glo' in a section titled 'Media He?' *Monday Conference* made it one of their topics for a live-to-air television debate, the book sold widely, and we imagined that the advertising world would rapidly see the error of its ways.

One day I had a phone call from an unknown writer who wanted to bring in his novel for an editorial opinion. Another carton arrived, this one full of meticulous pages written by Gerald Murnane, each an interconnected but self-contained segment, no paragraphs and no words wasted.

> If you could fill each square on a calendar with a picture instead of a number, and if each picture could show clearly some event or landscape or recollection or dream that made each day memorable, then after a long time and from a great distance the hundreds of pictures might rearrange themselves to form surprising patterns. *Tamarisk Row* is one such pattern.[9]

I wonder now about that pattern. Gerald Murnane and I worked together with the manuscript, sometimes in the office and occasionally at his house. Overnight he would rework segments and introduce new ones. This was one of those satisfying experiences for an editor that working closely with a fiction writer can be if things go well. My memory is of me becoming a kind of sounding board as the novel took its final form and the author's vision for the novel deepened. Gerald's memory is entirely the opposite.

Years later, when he had long been hailed as one of Australia's best novelists, we were both invited to speak at a public forum about editing and publishing. I spoke first and, without naming Gerald, described in loving detail my first experience of editing fiction, how much I had learnt, what a joy it had been watching the work unfold. Gerald then, without naming me, described the gruelling time he'd had with his first novel – how he'd been too obliging, agreed with too many of my suggestions and lived with a few things he was still unhappy about. My clumsiness and his inability to protect his work may have weakened *Tamarisk Row*. I can't tell even now. It still seems wondrous to me. But Gerald is a meticulous archivist and I suspect the record will show he was right. We were both feeling our way.

By the mid-seventies there were plenty of signs that non-fiction writing and publishing in Australia was becoming more receptive to ideas and starting to reach out for a general readership. There were books being published in genres and subjects that hadn't been there before.

John Mulvaney's *The Prehistory of Australia* had appeared in 1969 from Thames and Hudson, fully illustrated and designed in the style of their earlier titles on the Celts and the Anglo-Saxons. This not only signalled that Australian archaeology was on the move but that ancient tool cultures, rock art, and burial sites were of international significance. New excavations began to receive press coverage and a wide public, still being given an official assimilation-alist line about Aboriginal Australia, was made aware that the human occupation of Australia was consid-erably older and very much more complex than had previously been suspected by all but a few archaeolo-gists and anthropologists working in the field.

Much of the new work in Australian history and biography came from the university presses, and some of this writing was still rather conventional and lack-lustre. But Nelson in 1969 published Eric Rolls' *They All Ran Wild*, an account of the immense damage done to the environment by introduced species, and Michael Cannon's first volume in his illustrated his-tory of Australia for a general readership in 1971. Bill Gammage's *The Broken Years* appeared in 1974 from the Australian National University Press and Manning Clark's third volume of *A History of Australia* was published by Melbourne University Press in 1973. Heinemann published Ray Ericksen's autobio-graphical *Cape Solitary* in 1975 followed, in 1978, by his biography of explorer Ernest Giles.

Publishers and editors still tended to sit tight and wait for ideas to come to them. Hooker at Penguin was probably the most active at the time, commis-sioning Kenneth Maddock's *The Australian Aborigines*, Dennis Altman's *Homosexual: Oppression and Liberation*, which appeared in 1972, and Anne Summers was commissioned to begin work on *Damned Whores and*

God's Police, published by Penguin in 1975, the year Macmillan published Geoffrey Blainey's *Triumph of the Nomads*.

In 1973 Heinemann published the first cultural history of Australia, *From Deserts the Prophets Come*, by historian Geoffrey Serle, its cover a detail from Fred Williams' *Yellow Landscape*, its 'Contemporary Conclusion' Serle's observation of 'the high promise of the Australian dream and what History has made of it'. His title was taken from A.D. Hope's poem 'Australia'.

> Yet there are some like me turn gladly home
> From the lush jungle of modern thought, to find
> The Arabian desert of the human mind,
> Hoping, if still from the deserts the prophets come,
>
> Such savage and scarlet as no green hills dare
> Springs in that waste, some spirit which escapes
> The learned doubt, the chatter of cultured apes
> Which is called civilization over there.[10]

There were novels and plays and poetry being written in Australia by the generation that had grown up in the sixties, as I had, that needed a different kind of forum. That new literature seems to me, from this distance, to have really first started with Thea Astley's *The Slow Natives* in 1965, Peter Mathers' *Trap* in 1966, David Ireland's *The Unknown Industrial Prisoner* in 1971, then Frank Moorhouse's *The Americans, Baby* and Thomas Keneally's *The Chant of Jimmie Blacksmith* were published in 1972. Peter Carey's *The*

Fat Man in History appeared in 1974, and David Malouf's *Johnno* in 1975.

The centre of literary publishing had probably by the first half of the seventies shifted from Angus & Robertson, which was dealing with uncertainties caused by changes of ownership, to Queensland, where the University of Queensland Press, under American Frank Thompson, was publishing Murray Bail, Peter Carey, David Malouf, Rodney Hall and Thea Astley as well as a large poetry list. Macmillan had David Foster, Fay Zwicky, Jessica Anderson, William Marshall. Collins published Xavier Herbert's *Poor Fellow My Country* and Robert Drewe's *The Savage Crows* by the mid-seventies; Nelson had Christopher Koch, David Martin and Ruth Park. Thea Astley's *The Slow Natives* and *The Acolyte* had each won the Miles Franklin in 1965 and 1973. Jessica Anderson's *Tirra Lirra by the River* would appear in 1978. Shirley Hazzard, Patrick White, Morris West, Randolph Stow and many others continued to be published from London and New York with copies of their books imported into Australia.

Out of the new theatre and performance came writing from John Romeril, Jack Hibberd, David Williamson, Max Gillies, Alex Buzo, Kerry Dwyer, Alma de Groen, Helen Garner and others. John Tranter, Kris Hemensley, Laurie Duggan and John Forbes were some of the new poets. Younger women poets as strong as the previous generation of Gwen Harwood, Rosemary Dobson, Judith Rodriguez and Judith Wright were yet to be widely heard. Kate

Jennings' 1975 anthology of women's poetry, *Mother I'm Rooted*, was evidence that many women were writing although John Tranter's 1979 collection of *The New Australian Poetry* included only Vicki Viidikas and Jennifer Maiden.

This generation of new writers would have once left Australia and many would probably not have come back. After twenty-three years of conservative leadership, the election of the Whitlam government in 1972 felt like a seismic shift, a generational changeover that was long overdue – and was one of the reasons many expatriates gave for returning. The Australia Council's support for writers and artists was another. Set up by Liberal Prime Minister John Gorton under the guidance of Nugget Coombs, the Council's budget was boosted by more than half in 1973 by Whitlam, and its boards established. The arts in Australia felt themselves to be valued, and Australia, for once, seemed to the rest of the world to be ahead of the game.

Australia was a place many people felt optimistic about, and making a contribution to what we saw as its growing-up was part of it, for many of us. Throughout the sixties the numbers had been rising in universities and colleges. We had taken to the streets to put an end to Australia's involvement in the war in Vietnam. We'd voted in a Labor Government in 1972 and made it our own for the short time it was there – free tertiary education, the beginnings of a national health scheme, some progress on women's rights, the abolition of conscription, the establishment of the principle of Aboriginal self-determination and land rights, the recognition of China and a view of the region that included Australia. Whatever the failings of that government, and there was much disillusionment, the place felt as if it had been kick-started. The weakening of our links to Britain were perceptible as the ethnic and cultural mix of the place became richer. The children of the great waves of post-war immigration were enrolling in universities and tertiary colleges. The old smug mono-culture was fading fast. Australia was starting to look and sound like a more contemporary and cosmopolitan society prepared to find its own way forward.

Jim Davidson, who would become the next editor of *Meanjin* on the retirement of Clem Christesen, described on his return to Australia in late 1971 how the rising generation 'takes Australian culture in its stride and [may] shortly come to take it as its primary point of reference . . . they feel less and less constraint and pick and choose from what overseas has to offer . . . they regard Australia as a fully autonomous society . . . In short it's their metropolis.'[11]

Part Two

Often I have been camped in the swale of some
huge longitudinal dune and during the night,
the wind from some unusual quarter has
quarried down through several strata of sand
and revealed hidden layers of great antiquity –
say a thousand year old camp of the
Wangkanguru people. Or revealed the
geography of an older dune system which in
turn may cover the fossilised remains of a
Pleistocene forest. I have been looking on these
layered 'archaeologies', these gold and red piles
of different histories and systems as a metaphor
for the human psyche; the way each of us could
be seen as a walking many-layered world of
passions, ancestral memories, neuroses, genetic
patterns and ancient archetypes.

John Wolseley, Artist's Statement in Catalogue, *Paintings,
Lithographs and Sedimentary Prints from the Simpson Desert*,
Rex Irwin, Sydney, 1993, np

4

Making Books

The two black-and-white photographs I found recently we took of each other. It is high summer. Diana is sitting at a desk beside a large typewriter. This is one of the new IBM electric golfball machines with changeable typefaces. We used to say it could always be sold if we needed saving one day. She has her hair pinned up from the nape of her neck against the heat and is wearing the sundress with wide straps which was white like our one-room office. The other photograph is of me sitting cross-legged on the floor, deeply sun-tanned like young women used to be, and wearing a headscarf and a long dark dress. We are both laughing. It is February 1975 and the publishing house we didn't quite realize we were starting is four weeks old.

I found the photographs in a box labelled *Administration* by the university library that bought the company's papers fifteen years later, when things had gone wrong and the assets had all been 'acquired'. The last thing we did at the very end was pack the letters and papers from filing cabinets, the artwork from production drawers and watch as they were stacked into the truck with the university emblem on the side. Together, we visited the McPhee Gribble Archive, as it had become a few weeks later, and found it still in its old cartons in a huge wire cage waiting to be sorted. My memory is we couldn't speak and we went away into our separate lives. Diana's memory will of course be different.

Now, ten years on, the archive is in neat folders in the university library – the same library where I tried to write my Leavisite essays long ago and imagine the lives of scribes on rocky islands off the Irish coast. The library has the same smell and my feet make sounds I recognize on the stairs.

But when I work in the archive with its thousands of letters, telexes, file notes, photographs and the occasional shopping list and reminder about picking up the children or ordering more coffee from Grinders, I enter a world that exists somewhere else, in another time and space. I feel as if I have total recall. Letters that brought news of books sold to overseas publishers, from agents making offers we weren't expecting, from authors living in Greece or Paris for a year sending love to every member of staff by name, still produce exactly the same feelings of pride and pleasure they did at the time. A letter full of misunderstanding from someone we valued pro-duces the same pang of helplessness in me it did at the time. Flattering letters from overseas publishers courting us for as long as it suited them still make me want to laugh. File notes of difficult meetings towards the end where we were powerless to shape our fate still make me feel ill. The files act on me like the wardrobe into Narnia. I can only read them for a few hours at a time.

The boxes are brought to me on a cream trolley rather like those once used to ferry newborn babies to bedridden mothers in hospital. They are numbered and labelled and meticulously listed. They have their own printed Guide: Author files, Production files, Administration files, Press files and copies of every book we ever published. I immediately recognize the contents which, because current archival practice preserves authentic contexts, are still in the order we handed them over. I have to resist refiling letters that were misfiled long ago. A note from Helen Garner sits oddly in someone else's cover file – and I immediately think of the slightly dyslexic young girl we once employed because we liked her and she didn't wear lipstick, rather than the one with experience who did.

I am back in our first room in South Yarra, or the half underground bunker in Jolimont or the three-storey terrace house in Carlton or the shabby old warehouse painted pink in the back streets of Fitzroy. McPhee Gribble had four offices during its fifteen years and the spaces themselves seem to me to have produced different ways of working together and memories clinging to them that are mixed up with every aspect of our lives. The bunker we painted dark green with huge red lettering proclaiming our name, and this was where, when Hong Kong printers came to call, I hid my pregnant belly. The tall terrace was where we employed a student firelighter on winter mornings – and where the children were with us every day. The warehouse was where writers came to work with us often and where we did much of our best publishing.

But these are my recollections. I still have difficulty claiming even part of the story, and the stories are always shared ones. Fact and memory sit awkwardly together and story-telling carries its own distortions and momentum. One leads to another and then, sometimes, to a story that can't be told because it belongs too much to someone else. Balance and even-handedness are beyond me. Instead I try to find the words that ring true for me, which is the best I can do.

There is a list of names in the archive for the McPhee and Gribble partnership which Diana Gribble and I toyed with throughout 1974: names like Freewomen, Lois Lane and Associates, Copycats, Fat City, reflecting the times rather than any serious ambition – and the fact that two women who had become friends wanted to start something together but did not know yet what it would be. Women were inventing new enterprises, large and small, challenging our roles in existing organizations, intent on doing whatever we did differently from men and from our mothers' generation.

When McPhee Gribble began, independent publishers had been starting up around the world in all
kinds of fields, small, often radical presses producing
everything from polemics to poetry, instructions on
how to survive as single women to Chairman Mao's
Little Red Book. There was a climate of optimism and
activism, and a belief in books and the power of the
printed word to change things. There were enough
independent publishers in Australia to have to hire
chairs for the inaugural meeting of the Independent
Publishers Association which took place in the
carpark outside our office one warm evening that
first year.

A book production house making good-looking
books for established publishers to sell, as George
Rainbird had successfully set up in London a few
years before, was an obvious move for us.

Diana's background was in design and office management, mine was a total of four years in book
publishing and a brief exposure to management con-
sultancy. We would edit, design, print and deliver
into publishers' warehouses the kinds of books that
would bear the extra cost of out-of-house design and
manufacture. John Burchall at Heinemann had
encouraged the idea from the start and I would bring
with me three or four books to package for him and
the hope that other publishers would follow.

A vague dream ·of one day becoming a kind of
antipodean Hogarth Press hovered in the air, but the
reality was very different. At first there were just the
two of us in a rented room in a Victorian house in a

South Yarra back street with occasional use of another room when we needed to spread out artwork. In the days of long galley proofs and waxed repro, painstakingly Letrasetted headings and cover type, whole books were laid out on trestles around the room.

Within a few weeks our plans began to change. John Hooker, Penguin's senior editor, had the brainwave of commissioning a series of practical books for young children and had persuaded English Puffin Editor, Kaye Webb, not only to support the idea but to consider ordering them from Australia for English children – which had never been done before. Hooker's suggestions for first titles included 'Trainspotting' which may have helped. The series would be called *Practical Puffins*, handbooks for independent-minded children, aged 7–12 who 'like to do things for themselves'. They were to be written, illustrated, designed to finished art stage with translations in mind and Hooker would then try to put together an international print run.

The first six titles were then dreamt up, 'Trainspotting' was quietly dropped, and we all agreed, rather romantically, that the books should retail for no more than a dollar a copy 'so children could buy them with their own money'. Contracts followed describing what seemed to us a handsome and workable deal to produce six titles with an option to do more – for a minuscule royalty and a production fee. There were no precedents that we knew of, so we signed without a qualm. We had a cash flow and a publishing project which fitted our enthusiasms like a glove.

We took the idea of practical books for children most seriously. Our idea, which doesn't sound revolutionary now but was unusual in children's books then, was to speak directly to children as if they were autonomous and sensible, capable of making up their own minds, likely to be imaginatively engaged if the projects were good ones, bored if they weren't. A style of writing was developed by us through much drafting and discussion. Words like *fun* and *exciting* and *scary* were forbidden. So were exclamation marks. Warnings and any mention of parents and teachers were not allowed. The theory was that children were usually patronized and talked down to, so we eliminated dangerous ideas and tested everything on my two young children and Diana's nieces and nephews. Then the illustrator, David Lancashire, sketched from our photographs and rough texts the stages in making a cake, or a pair of stilts, or rose-coloured spectacles, or a surefire cure for hiccups. We watched closely as children mended bicycle tyres and made notes about how they handled tools. We hatched chickens in the office and grew mushrooms. We discovered that smells are molecules and could drift round corners, that they are strongest, as dogs know, close to the ground. We could identify cotter-pins and tenon-saws and make a sunstick to tell the time of day. We knew that if blindfolded people keep their mouths open slightly they can hear better. We became experts in arcane facts.

At first we simply drew on our own childhoods and those of people we knew, and combed old children's encyclopedias and annuals for ideas. We became adept at detecting where projects wouldn't work or had been lifted from somewhere else and passed on through book after book with the same flaw repeated. We tested our pages on classrooms of local school children and adjusted texts and layouts accordingly. We developed a strong sense of the differences between Australian childhoods and the much more protected American or more middle-class British versions, at least as they were represented in book form. We had in mind independent children who still had the basic freedoms we'd had ourselves, of exploring wild places and local neighbourhoods, of sleeping out under the night sky, of being able to ask friendly grocery stores for supplies of strong brown paper bags and cardboard boxes. *Practical Puffins* took over our lives.

In the files is a laconic Penguin memo dated 12 February 1976 from Bob Sessions, who had replaced me when I was moved on, to John Michie, who was about to be. 'First printing *Practical Puffins* is a fairly impressive 585,500 books.' While we'd been writing and illustrating, Penguin editors in Canada, the United States and the United Kingdom had all ordered large quantities from sample pages. Before long, editions with only slight modifications were being sold around the world and translated for the European and South American markets. Something like three million copies eventually sold worldwide, a precedent within the Penguin Group for inter-group sales, we were told, and some kind of record, perhaps, for Australian publishing.

The local response to the first six titles was startling. Television was not then a medium much interested in books – but it took to *Practical Puffins* in a big way. The combination of two young women and the idea behind the punchy little books for children which were selling worldwide, was a gift. That we had drawn so heavily on Australian childhood freedoms and attitudes appealed. And there were stories to be told. How one title, the innocuous *Body Tricks: to teach yourself* – full of things everyone in Australia remembered from the schoolyard: the nose crunch, the chopped thumb, the hypnotized arms, and the dead finger in a matchbox – was regarded as 'too weird' for the American market. How the Bishop of Norwich contacted the Chairman of Penguin objecting strenuously to our providing instructions on how to make a Ouija board for fortune-telling. This, we were astonished to discover, was considered deeply unsuitable because children might indeed get in touch with the devil. How Scholastic US offered us a very large order on condition that we dropped a joke that involved nailing a pair of slippers to the floor. We turned them down – an act which, in retrospect, perhaps could be seen as setting the tone for the company.

Practical Puffins taught us a way of working which stayed with us long after we had moved into mainly adult books. They infected the writing style of the office. Traces of them can be detected in the short paragraphs and direct speech of office letters, marketing materials, and cover copy. We were compelled to

develop systems and standards of research and originality which probably almost guaranteed their
success. We spent time on detail, on re-working until
we had what we were after. We fine-tuned the writing and editing always with the child-reader in mind.

Many years later, one dismal Saturday when our
profitability was under the microscope and the company was facing almost certain sale, we held an
all-day staff meeting where we attempted to talk
about cutting corners – producing books that were
seven out of ten, I think we called it. A few suggestions emerged from the discussion: doing less
face-to-face work with authors, accepting cover
designs that were not exactly what was wanted,
proof-reading once only . . . I thought about the
effort we'd put into those little books which was
probably the reason for their longevity and success
worldwide. Needless to say, we failed to convince the
staff to drop their standards and I doubt if they
believed we were serious anyhow.

The success of *Practical Puffins* also persuaded Ita
Buttrose, then editor-in-chief of the *Australian
Women's Weekly*, to take us on. With one of our
regular cashflow crises looming, Diana and I mocked
up some children's pages and trekked to Sydney in
our dark Melbourne clothes on a steamy day in 1977.
We watched as Ita, immaculate and pearly from
fingertips to toes, made up her mind to buy in less
than a minute. 'How much do you want a page?'
she asked. We hadn't done the sums and guessed too
low – but had many months of commissioning

stories, writing some ourselves and producing what we thought were three lively and mildly subversive children's pages each week. Ita liked them and her successor, Dawn Swain, tolerated them for a while. Then came the inevitable and furious phone call: 'Little boys don't *knit. Especially* little Italian boys.' Mary Pershall's story of Carlo, his father and the long magical scarf was the last straw.

Practical Puffins went on selling and reprinting for many years. We did editions in Greek and Turkish for non-English speaking Australian children as well. Penguin Group profits rose as a result. The Annual Report for 1975/6 announced that 'the cumulative net profit to 30 June 1976 was well ahead of budget' and that 'volume sales had increased significantly solely because of inter-group sales of the new *Practical Puffin* series'[1], and some people celebrated. But this is one of those stories that only half belongs to me. The rest belongs to John Michie, but by then I was his wife, and the story like everything in my life for all those years intersected with the office – so it has to be told as best I can.

By 1975 John had gone too far. I knew it and he knew it but there was still a lot of bullishness in the air at Penguin Australia, which was regarded internationally as the jewel in Penguin's crown and was making record profits. John had been invited onto the UK Board and was being spoken of in some quarters as the heir apparent. Supported by his Australian Board, he had plans to expand distribution into the region, and invest in increased local publishing. But the plans kept having to be shelved as demands to remit dividends escalated to shore up Penguin UK's profitability. Australia was to provide '66⅔ per cent of Penguin Group pre-tax profits in each of the years 1974–6', John had to advise the Australian Board in August 1974.[2] This meant capital expenditure in Australia had to cease. Late-night phone calls with the UK became more and more acrimonious.

One of the directors of Patrick-Intermarine was on Penguin's Australian Board and John, with the knowledge of his friend Ron Blass, Penguin's Export Director, but not of the UK Board, invested $150,000 of Penguin Australia's surplus cash with Patricks in an attempt to increase available profits. But in July 1975 Patrick-Intermarine collapsed and the money, on unsecured deposit, was lost.

It was not until February 1976 that directors of Pearson, Penguin's new owners, with Ron Blass in attendance, arrived at the Melbourne Hilton and demanded John's resignation. We knew it was inevitable. What we didn't expect was that *Practical Puffins* would be used against John, described as 'a sweetheart deal with your wife's company'.

My immediate response, with Diana's support, was determination to cancel our contract for future children's books. John's response, characteristically, to us and to those of his staff wanting to resign, was *not to give them the satisfaction of seeing us cave in*.

But, with the irony hindsight sometimes brings, we were caught in a kind of snare. It was the flow of royalties from *Practical Puffins* that now provided the income we needed to start publishing under the McPhee Gribble imprint. Essentially we'd been working until then writing and illustrating the books for a royalty and a production fee. Real publishing, finding the capital and the confidence to enter into a contract with an author, to licence their copyright, undertake to edit, design, print, promote and arrange distribution into bookshops around the country – that was another matter altogether.

Glen Tomasetti's *Thoroughly Decent People*, a perfectly poised folktale about pre-war Melbourne, precipitated us into becoming publishers in every sense of the word. Glen had arrived at our office one day late in our first year with the manuscript, for which she'd already had an offer from an established publisher. She had heard me launch Kate Jennings' anthology of women's poetry, *Mother I'm Rooted*, published by Outback Press, and liked the idea, she said, of women working together to publish books. My memory is that we tried to dissuade her. Glen was a singer and a folk historian and her eye for the detail and the texture of domestic life was unnerving – the bleached broom handle by the copper, the cork wrapped in lunch wrap in the picnic bottle of milk, the Sunday drive to the Dandenongs. Glen captured the small tragedies and stultifying gentility of daily life in Melbourne in 1934. We thought the book deserved much safer hands than we could offer, but Glen told us firmly that she'd ride her bicycle around the block to give us time to reconsider and we did.

For that, I shall always be grateful to her. We may have stayed in the protected zone of packaging books for other publishers for much longer than we did if we hadn't had a book as fine as *Thoroughly Decent People* to set up publishing systems for, to get out and sell. Keith Robertson designed an imprint 'look' of our own, a beautiful grid which could be adapted for all future hardcover books, and, for the cover of Glen's novel, an art nouveau design which might have come from the stained glass in the hall of Bert and Lizzie's East St Kilda villa.

Thoroughly Decent People was published in 1976, followed by Barry Hill's finely crafted short stories *A Rim of Blue*. Immediately their contracts were signed, the word was out and manuscripts began pouring in. Many looked as if they had spent a long time in bottom drawers or had done the rounds of other publishers, and some I'd seen before. Most were fiction and short stories despite the fact that very few publishers were interested in publishing unknown authors of fiction in the mid-seventies, and mocked fiction amongst themselves as more trouble than it was worth. John Hooker, a published novelist himself, stuck firmly to Penguin's policy of buying only occasional fiction titles previously published in hardcovers. Hooker joked that he wrote back to aspiring writers, 'We're okay for novels at Penguin, thanks.'

With two books of fiction to our name, the strong

men in publishing who liked to call by sometimes in the late afternoons with bottles of wine and kindly advice were already issuing warnings. Stick to packaging, do horse books or ballet books. Put together some recipes, get a preferably good-looking famous sheila to front them for you, and you'll sell 50,000 copies before anyone spots that they're not much good. *Anything but fiction*, they kept saying to us. Fiction was too much trouble, the authors too difficult, it didn't make money, and everything worth reading was imported anyway.

That wasn't how we saw it. There was writing and painting and performance in this new Australia that had different sounds and rhythms, that spoke, in voices and images that often had their origins in other parts of the world but were recognizably our own, to audiences who were here. Some of the work was self-conscious and some of it derivative but mostly it was finding its own forms that were uncompromising, sometimes confronting, rough around the edges maybe, and much more often concerned with changing the rules than with notions of great art. The post-1968 generation everywhere was making new art for audiences less constrained by form and function. Here what mattered more was that the best of it was unique, not fake, and not clamouring for the attention of anyone but ourselves. Women were writing out of their experience of traditional roles and the relationships they were now rejecting. A few men were struggling to put words to the horrors of Vietnam, based sometimes on their startlingly inarticulate letters home. The Whitlam government had lasted less than three years but the momentum of the changes it had set in train continued. Its sacking and its replacement by Fraser's Liberal Government in December 1975 produced much street theatre and a few conspiracy novels – but the politics of redefinition and inclusion were more interesting than the machinations of political parties. And, as always, artists and writers were heralding the changes and playing with them. McPhee Gribble became part of the shift and that was where we wanted to be.

One day in 1976, Helen Garner arrived at the Jolimont Lane bunker to tell us rather diffidently that she thought she might have written a novel. Would we take a look? And tell her *truthfully* what we thought. We each read copies of the manuscript of *Monkey Grip* overnight. And here was an original voice saying something that hadn't been said before under skies that were familiar from the opening lines.

> In the old brown house on the corner, a mile from the middle of the city, we ate bacon for breakfast every morning of our lives . . .
> It was early summer.
> And everything, as it always does, began to heave and change.[3]

The manuscript was a bit bumpy and awkward in places but there was no straining after effect, no literary flourishes, and I remember the pleasure, that physical shock that happens sometimes on first readings, and is, for me, an infallible sign of real writing.

After a desultory Christmas dinner with parents and a rich and conservative uncle, Nora gets on her bike and rides off down Studley Park Road back into her own life.

> I let go and flew down it in ecstasy, head thrown back, mouth open, feet at quarter to three, my bag of Christmas presents bumping against my back. The wind pushed at my front, the mudguards rattled so fiercely I thought the machine would fly apart. Down and round the wide metal curve, over the river almost invisible among humped trees, on my left the convent low down on its mediaeval banks, ancient trees shadowing its courts; and on to Johnston Street, slowing down from flight and back to legwork along the narrow road between the rows of closed factories.[4]

It was as if Nora was speeding into a present that many of us were trying to make sense of, inventing the rules as we went along, copping the hurt and the uncertainty that things would be alright.

The first reviews of *Monkey Grip* were mainly scathing and predictably sensational. 'Head Prefect of Tammy Fraser's old school at the centre of a storm about junkies and the counter culture,' reported the *Herald*. 'Immoral and sordid,' the *Australian* decided, and put my mother off reading the book for years. But those who did mostly loved it, sales in hardcovers topped 4000 copies in a few weeks which was big time then for an unknown novelist without a publicity budget. We had sent out many copies to reviewers and also to others we thought would talk about it, but that was it. Marketing hype in publishing had not yet been invented.

After *Monkey Grip* came *This Bed My Centre*, Ellen Newton's account of life in a nursing home. Ellen Newton was a pseudonym for Esther Levy, a former journalist, by then in her eighties, who had been encouraged in her critical writings by Nettie Palmer through a close correspondence beginning in the early 1920s.[5] Incarcerated in a nursing home with nothing more than a weak heart, Levy had written a cry for help to the Literature Board's project officer, Patricia Healy. Pat, friend to writers and to fledgling publishers, had arranged for Esther Levy to have a supply of pens and paper, and encouraged her to write a diary of her year.

> There's a hint of sun today in my small wedge of sky, but it does not touch my room. The sense of segregation is palpable . . . there's no sound of traffic passing by. Everything is negative. You never hear young people singing, speeding recklessly home from late parties . . . Never the sound of children's voices . . . Only spasmodic screeching a few doors away, that would send cold shivers down anyone's spine.[6]

When Pat Healy brought the manuscript to us for
an opinion, here, again, was a strong clear voice giving us, as the *Sydney Morning Herald* review later put
it, 'a chilling account of the subtle cruelties of nursing homes'.[7] The book sold well, was published in
the UK by Virago, where it also received enthusiastic
reviews – and Esther Levy found the strength and the
money she needed to arrange to check herself out of
the home and into a flat of her own.

By now McPhee Gribble had become, and would
remain, media fodder. *Practical Puffins* started it; and
the phenomenon, still unusual in the seventies, of
two women setting up a company together produced, as early as 1975, the first of the *Brains and
Beauty in South Yarra* headlines. Then the babies began
arriving: first Anna, Diana's daughter, and, six months
later, James, my second son. I don't think it occurred
to either of us to stop what we'd started although the
advice from many people was that of course we must.
Even John Michie and John Gribble who were our
chief supporters believed that we'd *blown it*. Running
an office and having new babies couldn't possibly
mix.

Instead we moved again to a large and seedy
Carlton terrace where we set up a nursery on the
ground floor – and McPhee Gribble kept growing
on the two floors above. We employed several kindly
young child minders, some with aspirations to *work
with books*, others to write – and Olga Lorenzo, who
came to us almost as soon as she arrived from Cuba,
did. Then we found Helen Brettagh and her baby

son and the remarkable Ron Hahn, a mother of six, who together in the back of the house and in its long narrow garden created a loving and creative place for children. This soon became known as the McPhee Gribble Childcare Department and other members of staff started having babies too. There were five at one count including Patrick O'Neil, son of publishers Lloyd O'Neil and Anne O'Donovan, who was producing her successful *Age Good Food Guide* from a room at the top of the house. We must have been the only publisher of the day to own two double pushers and a set of bunk beds – into which I would gratefully crawl with my baby son. 'James wants a feed,' would come a voice through the intercom, usually in the middle of meetings with embarrassed men.

Most people took the combination of children and office in their stride. A few of the men we dealt with, probably reminded of home by the noises off, looked irritated; others, having made their way through tricycles and wading pool to the outside dunny, would start talking about their own children. Someone told the media about us and the McPhee Gribble crèche and its occupants became instant role models. The politics of work-based childcare were just hotting up.

Our staff increased steadily. Our first part-time assistant was Julie Watts, who helped run the administrative corner of the room in South Yarra, then came Keith Robertson who laid out the books part-time, designed the covers, and stayed with us for many years. Keith brought with him, that first McPhee Gribble winter, an orphaned wombat that lived in a

box by the fire. Eventually we were able to employ
one or two maverick researchers, such as Michael
O'Rourke who played the Irish fiddle at lunchtime
and added greatly to our store of facts and projects as
the list of *Practical Puffins* grew to over twenty titles
during the first five years. Meredith Parslow, self-
styled high school dropout aged seventeen, turned up
one day and persuaded us to give her a trial. She
researched and pasted up dozens of books, designed
covers and catalogues, left and returned several times
and eventually became production manager.

The ages of the staff of fourteen or so ranged from
people in their late teens to Lois Freeman, our part-
time Pentecostal bookkeeper, heading for her sixties.
Occasionally we'd find books we'd published open at
offending passages as a gentle reprimand and each
Christmas the children would be given colouring
books featuring tongues of fire – which they loved.
Lois stayed with us for many years and somehow
weathered the gatherings at the coffee table where
people gossiped, smoked too much, wept and con-
fessed the details of the calamities and dramas that were
always striking someone down. We suspected Lois
prayed for us all a great deal and with good reason.

These were the years when marriages buckled
slowly and painfully and eventually collapsed, when
older children occasionally got into strife, when parents died, and when love affairs happened. One staff
member nearly ran away with an author's husband
and was talked out of it in the nick of time. Authors
confided their personal chaos sometimes too, and a

few went away to write about it. Somehow the office held us all. It was for as long as it lasted our safest place.

Thinking now about what it absorbed and what it gave, how we worked as a group, the ideas that we shared, the conversations, the confidences, the support offered whenever it was needed, the old cliché of the personal becoming the political springs to mind. This was how we all expected to work at a time of our lives when the public and private overlapped so much the division had no meaning. But that doesn't start to convey the complex web of relationships that held the place together.

The nature of the work we did, the relationship of author-and-publisher, must have been the starting point. We licensed authors' copyrights in order to find as wide a readership for their creative work as we could – but that doesn't come close to the reality either. Each book was different, each author needed something from us that was never articulated, nor could it be. We worked it out as we went. Trying to *put ourselves in the author's shoes*, was how we sometimes talked about it. But publishing also meant making choices, imagining readerships, visualizing the look of a page, being a filter, a means to a market. Often we were told what a powerful role this was – though it rarely felt powerful to us. Rejecting manuscripts was a task nobody enjoyed.

The pact implicit between employer and employee evolved as we grew. How shocked we were when we first heard ourselves described as 'they', and later, when we overheard someone to whom we gave occasional part-time work telling teenage children to make their long distance phone calls from the office rather than from home. We had a knack of nearly always choosing the right people, almost all of them inexperienced to start with. We couldn't have done what we did without them. The group was fundamental to the way we worked together – and so were all the threads of friendship.

Diana and I were close friends. We came from very different worlds. We learnt from each other until we could deputize on call, expert at reading the signs on each other's face, the tone of each other's voice. Diana once made us a gold star in the early days from foil and cardboard. We would prop it on a desk when one of us had weathered a formidable meeting and achieved results, or it would be slipped into a folder of artwork one of us was taking overseas – a private signal that we recognized in each other how hard it sometimes was and when courage was called for. We used to joke that we took it in turns to go in and out of panic – and for a long time I think that was true.

We started out with an ethos rather than a profit-motive, an idea rather than a money-making venture – which tougher heads would say was in the end our undoing. But for most of our fifteen years we had the luxury of a workplace where other priorities ruled. We became adept at dreaming up projects when the cash flow had dried to a trickle. We compiled handbooks and anthologies ourselves and wrote occasional children's stories for magazines and books under pseudonyms to bring in money. Holiday pay and annual leave loading was a regular nightmare and once or twice in the early years we paid wages on bankcard. All of us wore old clothes and drove small secondhand cars covered in dents and I don't recall anyone ever polishing a CV. We paid our staff what we could and more than ourselves if we had to. We earned around a school-teacher's wage most of the time. Everything else was re-invested in employing the people we needed in order to publish the books we wanted.

It was a way of working as remote now as the moon.

After a few years, probably on the strength of the international success of *Practical Puffins*, came the first of what were to be fairly regular and deeply distracting approaches from visiting British publishers or their Australian subsidiaries. *Why don't you join us?* became a familiar refrain. And for a while we might be tempted by an offer to co-publish, to produce a list, or to solve someone's marketing problems in Australia. Suggestions were sometimes made that some form of equity in the company should be acquired but we weren't actively seeking this. Most offers, we soon realized, came from visiting export directors or chief executives toying with the image of themselves as patron or partner or investor in ways that were probably rather gratifying when they were in Australia but unrealistic once they got home. And of course, sometimes after the weeks of follow up, most of these conversations came to nothing. McPhee Gribble on the other side of the world would recede rather rapidly.

Macdonald Educational, owned then by the British Publishing Corporation, was one company that sought us out at a point which seemed to make sense for them and for us. They visited the office, liked what they saw, were charmed by the visit to the Melbourne Club which one of them had hinted would help and which Diana had been able to arrange, and we were offered a deal. They were wanting to expand their Australian distribution and needed some 'school product' to do so. These books would, naturally, be supported in commercial quantities by the editors of Macdonald Educational (UK). Even then we knew that we should have our eggs in more baskets than Penguin's and an association with Macdonald might be the breathing space we knew would be needed to expand the staff, and to build our publishing programme. We were signed up to produce several series of storybooks and readers for primary school children to their pricing structure and formats. It sounded good. The figures seemed to work.

A couple of freelance writers, Roger Dunn and Garrie Hutchinson, who rented space from us, were commissioned, Jill Kitson and Judy Walker joined us to edit and research, Peter Freeman and Tony Ward became our chief illustrators, and we all became adept at producing stories that would readily translate for other markets. One of the requirements, this being the British Publishing Corporation with tentacles along the old routes of Empire, was that the artwork could be painlessly adjusted for skin colour. A simple plate change would produce red, brown and yellow-skinned children on demand for the Caribbean, African and Malaysian schools.

Then, quite quickly, what would become a familiar pattern emerged. The Australian distribution plans which had attracted us in the first place failed to materialize and the editorial support we'd briefly enjoyed in the UK began to evaporate. Sure enough, Macdonald Educational was about to be bought, sold and dismantled. But somewhere in the world I like to think there are still a few dog-eared copies of *My Trip in a Truck* and some of the other thirty or so titles we produced.

Shortly after *Monkey Grip*, a handwritten scrap of manuscript arrived at Drummond Street followed by its authors, two eighteen-year-olds calling themselves the Salami Sisters. Kathy Lette and Gabrielle Carey sang us their *Puberty Blues* song to persuade us to take them on. The manuscript was hilarious and hair-raising: the sex lives of two surfie chicks aged thirteen and fourteen, a story reeking of Vaseline, Marlboros and board wax.

We fell for the authors and gave them a contract on

the spot and then some rather firm editorial advice.
Many things about the book made us nervous. The
descriptions of gang-bangs and Coca-Cola douches
sounded terrifyingly flippant to us and their mockery
of other girls who were molls or nerds 'needed more
work'. The authors had to make it clear that shelter-
shed 'facts', like how to deal with a pregnant
girlfriend – 'your mate holds her while you hit her in
the stomach' – weren't on. Some of us had twelve-
year-old daughters who could head for the sand
dunes at any moment. Mine took the finished manuscript to her room, and after two hours of total
silence, emerged to say coolly that she'd found it very
well written. I was crushed.

After much reworking by the authors in the office,
who became adept at despatching some of our queries
with scathing notes in the margin such as 'If you don't
know what pulling off your horse means by now,
well . . .', the final version of *Puberty Blues* emerged in
all its glory. The Salami Sisters had parents too and I
wrote to them, at the authors' request, saying in the
most responsible tones I could muster how proud we
were 'to include your daughter in our publishing pro-
gram' and how brave their girls were 'to write so
frankly about their peer group'. I don't recall a reply.

Someone had the bright idea of writing to
Germaine Greer in Cambridge, champion of sexual
freedoms and rude words, hoping for a few powerful
lines for the cover. Greer eventually wrote back sternly
that she found the title 'fairly repellent' and thought
the manuscript contained 'the germ of a great comic

novel' but could do with a scholarly introduction by an
Australian anthropologist. But by then the book had
taken off – huge sales, film rights snapped up by Bruce
Beresford, and the Salami Sisters were hits. Kathy and
Gabrielle wrote to us later saying they 'were a little
worried that we now sound like goody-goody Bankie
chicks' – but we knew they never would. Perhaps
inevitably, Kathy and Gabrielle stopped speaking to
each other somewhere along the way and each went
on to become stars in their own fields. Meanwhile the
publishers kept getting letters from women of all ages
telling us that *Puberty Blues* had got it right – Cottesloe
Beach was just like that in 1944, so was Bondi in the
twenties – and *Puberty Blues* sold on and on.

Nineteen seventy-nine was the International Year of
the Child. It was also soon after the war in Cyprus and
a few years after the end of the war in Vietnam.
Australia's immigration policies were changing to
reflect where we were in the region, and although
European families continued arriving, others were
starting to arrive from Asia and South America. There
were 'boat people' from Vietnam coming to Australia
from refugee camps in Malaysia and Singapore.

Children in primary schools throughout the country had been invited by the Australia Council to
respond to a poster asking *How do you see your world?*
and teachers were encouraged to leave them to

respond in their own ways and in their first language. Over 10,000 children drew pictures, wrote poems and stories or short descriptions that revealed their lives. We found translators for entries in Turkish, Korean, Egyptian, Spanish, Vietnamese, Greek and Indonesian and a group of young people were invited to help us compile a book.

> Hello, my name is Bruce Coulter. I am thirteen years of age. I live in a hotel and go to the Kangaroo Flat Technical School . . . Let me bore you for a while, as I tell you about a normal weekday of my life . . .
>
> *Bruce, Marong, Victoria*

> I remember the pain and sorrow when my father left my mother. I was 5 and I still remember standing behind my mother watching my father go with his books under his arm.
>
> *Kirsten, Lavington, New South Wales*

> When I left my country on a boat to go to Thailand . . . we were short of drinking water then so everybody was thirsty and the children cried and howled . . .
>
> *Ly, Pennington, South Australia*

> I miss Polianka, my old wooden town in the mountains of Poland.
>
> *Janek, North Carlton, Victoria*

> When I grow up I hope to be an important person in the United States. I would like to visit the whole

world. I am going to marry a beautiful woman with hair like silk and skin like snow. My name is Con and I come from Greece. When I go to America my father is going to step up and say 'Son, I am proud of you.'

Con, Windsor, Victoria

Con and the others will be in their mid-thirties now. The stories they told – funny, tough-talking, heart-breaking – inspired *Our World*, a book that is still for me a clear snapshot of children living their lives in an Australia that was changing faster than ever, a slice of history at a particular moment in time.

Second novels, especially when the first has been a sensation and a success, are for many authors difficult things to write. There's pressure to deliver something even better and perhaps also a fear that everything you have had to say has been said before, that the material you were drawing on has been all used up and you haven't got it in you to start again. Publishers are under pressure to deliver again, too, as if to prove the first time wasn't a fluke.

After Helen Garner won the National Book Council Award for *Monkey Grip* I was taken aside by an elderly Arthur Phillips, who had defined the cultural cringe and its mirror image, the strut, in *Meanjin* in 1950,[8] and of whom I was in awe. He told me how much he admired *Monkey Grip* but how concerned

he was that Helen was too young to win a major literary prize. It would be bad for her. It could do her
writing no good. She must keep a low profile for the
next few books. I hadn't the heart to tell him she was
thirty-four years old nor did we see our role as turning authors on or off.

Helen was by then living in Paris and postcards in
her fine bony handwriting often arrived at the office.
She was writing, she said, first stories, then it seemed
that a novel was under way. 'I am launched . . . I
daren't mention the subject matter to anyone or even
really say "I am writing a novel" for it may evaporate
at any moment.'[9]

A little later, in 1979, Diana and I were in London
for a few weeks staying in a reeking ruin near
Victoria Station, displaying our wares to agents and
publishers and barely sustained by telexes and postcards from the office with news of the children. We
missed them painfully. There was a card from our
editorial assistant, Veronica James, whose daughter
Clare was in the Childcare Department too. 'Anna
has had a haircut (not much off). Children just back
from Myers and played on the escalators.' We longed
to go home. Then a telegram arrived from Helen
asking if we could come to Paris where she had two
copies of the new manuscript waiting for us.

We read *Honour* in silence all afternoon on iron
seats at opposite ends of the Tuileries. Then Helen
came to the Hotel Esmeralda where we drank whisky
and talked miserably for hours before trailing back to
London having done the only possible thing: told

Helen the truth – that the first draft of *Honour* didn't work for us. There's a telex in the files to the Carlton office dated 3 July 1979: 'Very rushed trip to Paris. Helen is fine but her book is rotten.' We thought she'd go to another publisher and that we'd lose her for good.

Helen came back to Australia the following year and a new version of *Honour & Other People's Children* was published by us in 1980. The two novellas are among the very best accounts of the pain adults inflict on young children in their blundering attempts to rewrite the rules.

> They sat helplessly at the table, survivors of an attempt at a family, while the little girl wept aloud for the three of them, for things that had gone wrong before she was born and when she was only a baby, for the hard truth which they had thought to escape by running parallel with it instead of tackling it head on.[10]

Helen was living nearby and had been a friend for a long time. She called in often, arriving briskly. We'd discuss new shoes or bands and exchange instalments in the stories of our lives. She'd usually depart as fast as she'd come, leaving behind her a chapter or a short story or a letter in an envelope. Later that day or the next we'd talk on the phone. Several years after *Honour* was published, when she was writing *The Children's Bach*, a note from her was waiting for me one afternoon when I got back to my desk.

I'm terribly pleased that you like the stuff I sent you. I care a lot about what you think (Di too) and trust you both, ever since that ghastly day in Paris when you so sensibly and correctly knocked back that botch up I had presented you with. Actually until this very moment it had never occurred to me how *disappointed* both of *you* would have felt. So thanks for sticking by me. This means a *lot*.[11]

It meant a lot to us too.

The list was taking shape by the early eighties – fiction and non-fiction, children's and adults' books, both literary and 'popular' – the mix was essential. The Australian market was too small and export opportunities too rare to sustain a literary list or a list with a special focus like the one Virago had succeeded in establishing so well in London. I don't think either of us would have wanted to specialize in any case.

Instead, Sisters, a feminist book club and occasional publisher of women's writing, had been established in 1979 by five women publishers. Each of us had our own publishing operation so we didn't have to persuade anyone else that books by women were a whole new market. Most publishers were, at this time, fairly antagonistic to the notion. Sally Milner, Joyce Nicholson, Anne O'Donovan and Diana and I pooled our resources, which were mainly our labour, to bring out occasional volumes of fine feminist poetry and stories that could not yet be published commercially.

Sisters employed Clare O'Brien and had an editorial board which now reads like a who's who of Australian feminism of the day. In Australia we invited Edna Ryan, Eva Cox, Faith Bandler, Carmel Niland, Judith Wright, Elizabeth Riddell, Drusilla Modjeska, Dany Torsh, Fay Zwicky and many others to join the board. In the UK there was Carmen Callil and Anne Chisholm, and Paula Weideger in the States. We had links to Virago, the Women's Press and small feminist lists and offered a range of titles by mail order. Jean Bedford's *Country Girl Again* was one of the first titles Sisters published in 1979, followed by Beverley Farmer's first novel *Alone* in 1980. Emily Hope's *The Legend of Pope Joan* and collections of poetry by Jennifer Strauss, Rosemary Dobson, Antigone Kefala, Jennifer Rankin and Judith Rodriguez and others, followed over the next few years.

Sisters' fiction and poetry publishing sold in numbers that surprised even us. Much of it reprinted and was enthusiastically reviewed – and probably gave rise to the curmudgeonly rumours which started circulating during the early eighties that there was a female literary mafia out to destroy the work of men by giving preferential treatment to women's writing.

We were sometimes given a hard time by authors who believed we had an obligation to publish, that editing should be a collective enterprise or not at all. We worked rather differently. We kept Sisters going for the next four or five years as best we could in our spare time, packing orders at weekends and editing late at night. One author was only persuaded at the eleventh hour to relinquish some hundreds of adjectives she didn't need. With the book due at the printers the next morning, Diana and I spent the evening in the office with scalpels chopping from the pasted-up pages adjectives which would re-appear each time the floor was swept for years afterwards.

When feminist publishing was no longer considered marginal according to mainstream publishers, we were able, with some relief, to leave them to it. We quietly closed the list and celebrated with a Paterson's cake iced with *Sisterhood is Powerful* in big letters. McPhee Gribble had published women's writing since the start and would continue to do so simply whenever it seemed to us the most creative and original writing at the time.

I still have some of the books Sisters offered through its bookclub, kept on a bottom shelf, behind the sofa, because I expect I'll never read them again, a row of books written by women in the seventies and early eighties. I keep them because they remind me of those years when we thought we were finding ways to talk to each other that hadn't been there before. Or perhaps we didn't know where to look. We were very sure of ourselves in the days before some of the words became straitjackets and our lives seemed not to fit the new certainties any better than they had the old ones we had tried so hard to leave behind.

In the few years since we began, the Australian publishing landscape changed a good deal. Many of the liveliest books were coming from independent publishers despite their shared difficulties with distribution. In Western Australia, Fremantle Arts Centre Press published after investing a great deal of editorial time in what would become the most successful autobiography of the decade by an unknown veteran of the First World War – Albert Facey's *A Fortunate Life*. We had signed some of the best books by younger authors of the day. We were commissioning non-fiction and we were starting to buy rights to some American non-fiction titles, adapting them for Australia. Established writers were still tentative about coming to us but their agents were putting out feelers.

But perhaps the biggest shift in the early eighties was that Australian fiction had come to be considered sexy and fashionable and worth the risk. It was selling well; new and established authors were producing novels in increasing numbers. It was regarded as a smart move when James Fraser persuaded friend and author Robert Drewe to leave Collins with him, and, using Fraser's superannuation, together published Drewe's highly successful *The Bodysurfers* in 1983. The University of Queensland Press published Thea Astley's *An Item from the Late News* in 1982, Olga Masters' *Loving Daughters* in 1984, and Peter Carey's *Illywhacker* in 1985. David Malouf had moved to Chatto & Windus and Carmen Callil, and *Fly Away Peter* was published in 1982. Murray Bail's

Homesickness published in 1980 and David Foster's *Moonlite*, 1981, both appeared from Macmillan. Authors of Australian fiction were starting to be valued, and to change publishers. There was competition that hadn't been there a few years before.

Meanwhile, our three-storey terrace house at 203 Drummond Street had been declared unsafe for offices because the floors and doors weren't fire-rated. Carlton had become rather fashionable, the children had climbed the fire escape with no clothes on once too often and been banished to pre-school, and we'd moved to a hideous old warehouse in the backstreets of Fitzroy in inner Melbourne. This had in previous incarnations been several kinds of sweat shop. Under the floor were thousands of inner soles, the place was hung with rows of fluorescent lights, and an industrial heater blasted hot air with such force that it had to be turned off when the phones rang. But we painted the walls pale pink, did clever things with the lighting, and had by now acquired a large enough 'stable' of authors for their photographs to line the stairwell in the manner of the walls of Farrar, Straus & Giroux and Jonathan Cape.

Next to the stairs we made a sitting area with a big coffee table surrounded by armchairs and old sofas. Here the coffee flowed and people talked. The editors, who included at various stages during this time

Michael Langley, Sophie Cunningham and Sue Hines, then later Judith Lukin-Amundsen, Sandra Meredith and Joan Grant, had a long carpeted room and a Macintosh Plus with one megabyte of RAM all to themselves upstairs. Diana and I worked in two tiny offices on either side of the front door and the rest of the space we filled with bookshelves and white-paper-covered trestles – a production department, research and reception areas.

The warehouse was made for book launches and parties and we had them often. The McPhee Gribble Christmas Party had been a fixture since year one and at 66 Cecil Street, Fitzroy, they became huge and desirable. They were determinedly unglamorous and as inexpensive as we could make them – always BYO and catered for by us at the nearby markets. The guest list was regularly dissected, occasionally and dramatically culled, but it kept on growing until we were spilling out onto the street on hot nights – that usually ended in a mass descent on to the Penang Affair in nearby Brunswick Street.

We gave good parties, we published some of the best books of the day, we were proud of the morale in the office, but we were still deeply restricted by regular cash flow crises and poor distribution. Every independent publisher in a country the size of Australia with its markets thinly spread has still to cobble their distribution together state-by-state like we did. The other alternative, an agency arrangement with a large overseas-owned publisher, is expensive and the suspicion is always there that your own books

take second place, last out from the rep's bag and least
understood.

Brian Johns, former journalist and political staffer,
had joined Penguin as Publishing Director in 1979.
There he had quickly broken the old taboo on publishing original fiction at Penguin and his list
included much new writing in paperback and hardcovers. He was publishing fiction from established
writers such as David Ireland, Blanche d'Alpuget,
Thea Astley, Elizabeth Jolley, and was commissioning
widely as well. There was Richard Haese's *Rebels and
Precursors*, a history of the modernists in the John and
Sunday Reed circle at Heide, which had included
Nolan, Boyd, Tucker, Hester, and Vassilieff; there was
Henry Reynolds' account of Aboriginal Australia *The
Other Side of the Frontier*; Bernard Smith's autobio-
graphy *The Boy Adeodatus*; and Brian had just signed
John Bryson to follow the 'dingo baby' case, when
Lindy Chamberlain was charged with murder over
her baby's disappearance at Ayers Rock.

Brian called women *boilers* and somehow got away
with it, believed the One True Faith left the rest of
us heathens, and had a habit of ringing at twelve and
insisting on lunch. But he was driven by what he
liked to call *the force of ideas*, and quickly became a
close friend and supporter of Diana's and mine. Friday
nights at the office were almost invariably times spent

arguing politics, religion and feminism, suggesting books and authors for each other over bottles of red wine. We ought to have been locked in competition but instead we admired each other's lists, relished each other's successes, and recognized we shared the same big idea.

In 1983 Brian proposed a co-publishing arrangement between the two companies which seemed to all of us to provide McPhee Gribble with the best of both worlds and Penguin with an even more expanded list. As he said later in an interview:

> It is undeniably true that we didn't have available to us at Penguin in Australia the reprint and takeover opportunities that Penguin elsewhere in the world had . . . And I was interested in Australian publishing, not just in Penguin Australia's publishing. I knew the great advantage we had at Penguin was our marketing and distribution machines, and it would be good for McPhee Gribble to have access to that and for Penguin to have a solid flow of additional books.[12]

The arrangement that Brian and Managing Director Trevor Glover had come up with meant that Penguin would buy from McPhee Gribble whole print-runs, the quantities to be established in consultation with Brian rather than having to go through Penguin's rather laborious meeting structures. Glover, who had taken over from John Michie in 1976, and had appointed Johns, was a rare Englishman who was enthusiastic about Australia and Australian publishing.

The terms were stringent: we would receive 31 per cent of the retail price, royalty paid, with marketing and promotion support to a level to be negotiated book by book. In exchange, a selection of our publishing would appear in Penguin covers and paperback formats at Penguin's retail prices. *McPhee Gribble/Penguin* became the imprint.

The new arrangement was announced with much fanfare and enthusiasm on both sides. The authors were happy. The media was impressed. The Pearson Annual Report in the UK described the arrangement with Penguin as 'an exclusive packaging arrangement'. They were right although that wasn't how we thought of it. We still saw ourselves as autonomous and independent. We financed the publishing, contracted the authors and worked closely with them; our attempts to develop new markets for Australian books went on as before. But most of our books now looked like Penguins, were often reviewed as Penguins, and much of our stock in the Ringwood warehouse was owned by Penguin.

Nor did the irony of what we were doing occur to me – even, all those years before, having gleefully removed the boomerangs from Penguin's own Australian list. The co-publishing agreement seemed to have everything going for it. It gave us a small but predictable cash flow which we'd never had before. The authors were the main beneficiaries, and this meant a lot to us. They now had full access to what Penguin's Marketing Director liked to describe as their *Rolls-Royce distribution service*. At the same time they had all the loving care and attention to detail small publishers like McPhee Gribble could bestow, and most large publishers couldn't – or wouldn't.

But, as Diana said later, it wasn't a Rolls-Royce we needed at this time, it was an old ute. And one that belonged to us.

For the next few years, while Trevor Glover and Brian Johns were at Penguin Australia, the arrangement worked smoothly and we concentrated on publishing books. Our list grew steadily, the books sold well, and reprinted at the same rate as Penguin's own. But our margins were minuscule and almost as soon as we signed the co-publishing agreement, advances for authors in Australia, as they did elsewhere, began to rise steeply. We gradually became aware of how vulnerable we were.

5

The Other Side
of the World

Home by the late seventies was an old bank building on the waterfront at Williamstown on Point
Gellibrand which faced the city across Hobsons Bay.
Williamstown was one of Melbourne's oldest ports,
where convict prison hulks once anchored, where
hopefuls in search of gold disembarked then made
their way overland to the goldfields of Ballarat and
Bendigo. Williamstown, I discovered, was also where
many of the Gaelic-speaking victims of the Highland
Clearances and the Irish and Scottish famines were
first quarantined before being allowed to set foot on
the land that had taken them months to reach. My
father's family from Skye was amongst them – but I
did not know that then. At Point Gellibrand stood the
Time Ball Tower built in 1852 to replace the colony's
first wooden lighthouse. Here a brass ball would be
dropped at midday each day, so that the growing city
of Melbourne and ships at anchor could set their
clocks and navigational instruments to local time.

From our upstairs windows we could watch the huge container ships moving up the Bay into the channel to the mouth of the Yarra River and the docks. Occasionally we'd recognize the names of the ships from shipping documents and know they were carrying books from Britain awaited by Australian readers. Books had been shipped from north to south like this from the beginning of the colonies and not a lot had changed. They would be cleared through customs by shipping agents then trucked to publishers' warehouses and from there sold into the bookshops. The time from publication in Britain to publication in Australia was now usually faster and even sometimes simultaneous if well planned for a major promotion. But usually the books sailed when they were ready, as useful additions to print-runs needed in the UK.

Only rarely did finished copies of Australian books leave Australian ports for sale overseas. The incentive to develop overseas markets for books made in Australia was never really there for the overseas-owned publishers whose parent companies took the view that export was better done out of London – as it always had been, along the routes of Empire. Instead, those Australian publishers who wanted to build up new markets concentrated on trying to sell rights to overseas publishers.

Selling Australian books to the rest of the world is expensive, arduous and only rarely successful – but it is an essential part of what a publisher does. For those publishers without the international links that foreign ownership or equity provides, nothing can replace the face-to-face contact with agents and publishers year after year in New York, London and Frankfurt. And the only way for McPhee Gribble to do this was in one gruelling round-the-world buying and selling trip each year.

At first Diana and I shared the load and went together. The fathers brought the children into the office each day and the staff sent us news and drawings. We hated leaving home. For a few years we took it in turns. Then later as the company grew and our roles became more differentiated, Diana took on the administrative load, the finance and production side and I concentrated on building the list and establishing a rights and export market for our publishing.

Most of our efforts overseas in the early years went into trying to place our children's books which had some chance of sharing print-runs in quite large numbers. Australian non-fiction, unless it was pitched at the tourist market – *Hang-Gliding for Beginners* or biographies of international sporting heroes – had little chance of being placed. Books on Aboriginal art and culture were beginning to be of interest to German and a few American publishers but the British still looked at them blankly. Lonely Planet was expanding its export markets steadily in ways no other publisher could match with guides for the budget travel that was spreading across the globe. Australian non-fiction, books of ideas, of history, of philosophy, of cultural or political or economic analysis had not yet made any kind of international mark. The experts we listened to were still largely imported.

Fiction, on the other hand, 'travelled' and by the early eighties was being published in greater numbers in Australia than ever before. But it was a long time before the fiction any Australian publishers produced was taken seriously by overseas publishers. 'Of course, we'd have to cost in having the book re-edited,' said a London publisher to me after she'd agreed to read one of our novels which had been well-received in Australia a few months before. The burden of the reputation that preceded us, that Australian novels were badly edited, I tracked down eventually to a fiction list of six or eight titles that had been cobbled together at least a decade earlier by publishers who didn't know what they were doing – or maybe they did – and an American carpetbagger had jobbed them off to a wholesaler. These largely unedited novels had been barely noticed in Australia but they were often mentioned to me disparagingly by New York agents and publishers. They would reach onto their shelves, some of them, and pull out a ten-year-old copy to show me exactly what they meant about weak editing. I could only agree.

Later when our books were welcome and deals were on the table, some American agents and publishers still felt free to suggest changes even after publication in Australia. The implication seemed to be that Australian books were unfinished. Their enthusiastic reception had been a useful kind of dress rehearsal for the real thing.

Some of the comments were legitimate, reflecting as they did cultural differences or misreadings, but most were not. Sometimes they were structural; sometimes they were merely cosmetic, such as suggestions to Americanize the characters' names. One US agent wanted us to persuade Tim Winton to change the ending of *That Eye, the Sky* which was collecting awards in Australia as we spoke. That there were real live authors crafting original work at the end of this long commercial chain sometimes came as a surprise.

In Britain, the problem we faced was rather different, and more about the anxieties of a shrinking market for their own literary fiction. Books previously published in Australia were regarded as unprofitable because the export market had already been eroded. No matter that most novels from British publishers in Australia sold well under a thousand copies – the assumption was that without Australia nothing was viable. This encouraged a few British literary publishers to comb Australian publishers' lists and those from the Literature Board of the Australia Council for the 'big names', a handful of authors who could be enticed to leave their Australian publishers and be published back into Australia from England.

The search for The Great Australian Novel, abandoned in Australia in the late sixties, still seemed to be alive and well in Britain. It was not inconceivable, was the implication, that a next generation Patrick White or Christina Stead might emerge in Australia, but they would need saving from their hopeless publishers. An author unfortunate enough to be published first in Australia would have been burdened with poor editing, poor production, endings that weren't neatly tied up. The condescension and complacency were maddening and sometimes hard to bear. We spent fortunes on phone calls back to the office and to home to keep our spirits up.

The fallacy that the UK market could not be viable if a book had first been published in Australia was almost impossible to dislodge. It was about our right to an export market, but it was also about a more fundamental cultural struggle. Already many of the conglomerates were arguing for world rights across all markets in the push towards the consolidation of copyrights in anticipation of electronic convergence. We were arguing the opposite – that it was better for authors and the books to have separate contracts and, if necessary, separate publishers in the British, American and Australian markets.

A fierce debate waged all through the eighties and, ironically, it was Carmen Callil, one of British publishing's most powerful figures, who happened to be an Australian, who led the fray. Throughout her time in publishing, Carmen was intensely interested in Australian writing and became David Malouf's publisher when she moved to Chatto in 1982, positioning him brilliantly. Diana and I had met Carmen in London when we both started to travel in the early years. Carmen established Virago from the outset as a publisher of books by women, reintroducing modern classics that had been neglected as well as contemporary feminist writing, whereas McPhee Gribble was intent on building a general list. Carmen and Ursula Owen, when they worked together at Virago, were regarded by many as direct equivalents of Diana and me and in some ways they were.

When she acquired *Monkey Grip* for the Virago list, Carmen became a friend and ally. An Australian of Lebanese-Irish parentage, she was one of a number of now well-known expatriates who had left Australia in the fifties and early sixties. She had arrived in London in 1960, started Virago in 1972, made her mark internationally, and had not returned to live in Australia. She was Virago's Managing Director until 1982 when she became Publisher of Chatto & Windus and The Hogarth Press. Carmen and I have weathered similar storms and corporate upheavals, we have been bought and sold and survived, I suspect, only because we're both sustained by the books and authors we've published. Our lives have been curiously parallel, in some ways, at opposite ends of the earth.

We argued often about the splitting of rights and markets. Carmen believed that good editing can happen anywhere, that the clout of the publishing house in the world, the company an author keeps on lists such as she was in charge of at Chatto, with writers such as Michael Holroyd, Angela Carter, Toni Morrison, and A.S. Byatt, were more important than anything else a publisher had to offer. Many authors, I am sure, would still agree with her. With the choice of North American, European and English literature, budgets much larger than ours and a British market of sixty million, she could, I know, have picked the eyes out of Australian lists, including ours, any time she liked – but she didn't. We argued that British publishers should buy British rights from us and that authors were better heard and supported in the development of their work if their editing and their writing reflected their primary audience. Then, ideally, once an author was well established and widely sought after in the world, there should be editorial input from each major market with the author always in charge. I don't believe I ever convinced Carmen, although Virago did regularly buy titles from us – and I know this helped establish our credibility in the US market.

Carmen's letters and telephone calls from the start were characteristic combinations of affection, tart advice and tough bargaining. 'Darling, you haven't *understood* what's involved in this sort of thing . . . If we take only 10 per cent, [she was arguing for 15 per cent of *Monkey Grip*'s royalties in America on top of the US agent's cut] we'll almost certainly lose,' she wrote when we were struggling with agreements. She always won. She taught me much, and she's a friend.

We were not only arguing about selling Australian books – we were arguing about buying rights to those American and even British titles that we knew we could publish better in Australia than was currently the case. Splitting rights in the four main English language markets, the UK, North America, Canada and Australia, felt to us like the logical next step in the long slow development of an international publishing industry that recognized the benefits of accommodating cultural differences. How could a British editor always know what Australian readers wanted to read? Why should Australian readers have to wait for a British editor to buy books for the UK market with Australia attached? Our reading tastes were sometimes quite different. As Australia changed throughout the seventies and eighties, we were less like England than we'd ever been. Canadian independent publishers were arguing along similar lines in their attempt to differentiate themselves from the US market. We were all envisaging a more responsive and sophisticated international publishing environment – in place of what was already on the horizon, a global publishing and media marketplace with local differences flattened out, world rights for those authors whose copyrights would be valuable commodities in the future.

And, in any case, McPhee Gribble argued, publishing only Australian authors was an unnatural state of affairs. No serious London or New York publisher published only their own books – or not one worth the name. All we were contemplating was the ability to apply Australian filters to international writing, to use Australian noses to detect bestsellers, Australian ears for regional voices. Why should Australian readers be denied a new novel from an East Timorese writer, say, because an English editor didn't think readers in Britain would be interested?

What we were proposing was good for authors, good for readers, good for publishing. We argued the case at every turn to agents, on public platforms, in the press. It felt nonsensical to have to buy American books through London agents and publishers rather than by dealing direct. But we were already up against forces that wanted a simpler marketplace where maximizing profits in the short-term was the guiding principle. On my first visit to Simon & Schuster in New York, it occurred to me that the McPhee Gribble offices would occupy no more than the foyer. Now I can see that we were chipping away, from our tiny base, at the coalface of postcolonial publishing relationships, with our bare hands.

In the early eighties, I sometimes found myself following in Carmen's footsteps around the New York agents. When we were in town at the same time, she was always generous with introductions even though she knew my message was the opposite of hers and the last thing she believed in. The New York agents loved the drama of it all. Ginger Barber was one of Carmen's good friends and someone we sparked off from the start. 'Wait a minute,' Ginger said to me in her lovely southern belle voice over a Japanese lunch near Madison Square one day. 'Carmen will kill me, but what you are saying is worth a page in my Filofax.' Filofax pages were thirty cents each then so

I was gratified. No American agent had yet been to Australia. Most told me I was the first Australian publisher they'd ever had a meeting with. Of course they'd adore to deal direct with Australia and with McPhee Gribble in particular.

Carmen Callil visited Australia often and still does, remaining sensitive to its changes, protective of its differences and knowledgeable about Australian writing and politics. She demands updates on election day. We raged together as Thatcherite policies belatedly started to bite in Australia and when the referendum on the Republic was lost. Few of her colleagues in British publishing would have considered Australia likely to generate ideas worth sharing. Or be able to see a political culture that might have some bearing on their own. Inconceivable that Australia, sharing some ancestral memories, open to others in another kind of postmodern universe, might be more than just a convenient market for export sales. The two-day annual visit to check on the Australian subsidiary that had become the norm by the early eighties didn't expose them to much of interest. But I'd see Carmen across the grass at most of the bi-annual Writers' Weeks in Adelaide, a tiny argumentative figure in a large hat, and my spirits would lift.

It was a long while before English editors and agents rather than export directors started coming to Australia looking for authors to publish, but in October 1981 we had a letter from Matthew Evans at Faber. 'In mid-November Robert McCrum will be coming to Australia on a scouting trip. I think this may be the first time a British publisher has been to Australia with the specific purpose of talking to Australian publishers and trying to buy rights to Australian books . . . He'll give you a ring.'

But why would he when Australian authors were queuing at his door to offer their books to a list as well established as Faber's? We kept spotting him at lunch in Carlton deep in conversation with someone else's authors. It would not have occurred to Robert or to Matthew Evans, his Chairman, I'm sure, that he was striking at the heart of what we were trying to do. This was how the world worked and made commercial sense. We tried and tried to sell rights to Faber but, without Australia attached, we were firmly told, the numbers 'didn't work' for them.

Every culture has its own mix of voices that read the way they do because they are embedded in accent, in place, in history. The connections and dislocations of the past, the predilections and prejudices of the present filter through the voices of writers – and give world literature in English its great richness and variety. This is what is at risk if subtle differences are flattened out in global media, in film, in literature, in theatre.

Australian writing in the world has always had a hard time of it – and now more than ever before, perhaps. Our accents are mocked or misheard. Our voices are not strong because the range of Australian writing is so restricted into other markets. Our writers are rarely able to be part of the world's great literary and intellectual conversations. As the stakes get higher, writers in all media are starting to feel the pressure to iron out the differences, remove the idiosyncrasies that link creative work to its place of origin. Some of the next generation of Australian writers, irritated by their local sales figures, or in response perhaps to contracts acquiring world rights, are again, as many writers did in the fifties and sixties, consciously shaping their Australian material for readers in the northern hemisphere. The reader in their head is *over there*.

Especially to the English ear, the idiom of most Australian novels was, and still is, read as rather raw, vernacular or too 'flat' – not musical or 'exotic' in the way of Indian or Caribbean or Irish or Scots writing in English. Australian novels sometimes sprawl or approach the reader from surprising angles. They tend not to be given to dashing flourishes of authorial coerciveness. They are not usually stylistically tidy or even noticeably shapely. Their settings, if urban, are not usually 'foreign' enough to give readers a sense of having escaped into another world; if rural or outback they no longer conform to the reassuring stereotypes of 'Banjo' Paterson or Arthur Upfield.

Australian readers seem to me to be able to move effortlessly between regional voices within English, American, Canadian and Australian literatures as well as other literatures in English from India, the Caribbean, the West Indies. Our exposure to a diverse range of writing from the English-language world is wider than that of most American and English readers. Few English readers have read much recent Australian writing because there is so little in English bookshops and almost none in the libraries, and this is compounded by time lags and lacklustre reviews. English readers visiting Australia for the first time might read Christina Stead and Patrick White, then perhaps David Malouf, Rodney Hall and Elizabeth Jolley, who could be said to write *into the imagined space between the two hemispheres*, long before the nuances of Kate Grenville or Robert Drewe or Christos Tsiolkas or Kim Scott would start to work for them.

By the early 1980s it was different altogether in America. Even in the fifties Patrick White had found his American publishers more comprehending and enthusiastic than his British publishers – he was once famously asked to explain what *The Tree of Man* was *about*. American agents and publishers, having overcome their nervousness about our capacity to edit, were more open to Australian writing, perhaps because of their own range of regional and ethnic voices. Australian writers were merely a curiosity at first, but if they had something unusual to say or a story to tell that hadn't been heard before, and particularly one which might translate into serious sales, and was, as they say, *commercial*, they were welcomed enthusiastically. Reviews were usually generous and curious rather than bored and carping.

Garner had all of her books published in the States in the eighties, and while British reviewers and publishers took longer to respond, American reviewers seemed to 'hear' Helen's prose from the start and were open to it. The *TLS* had headed its review of the 1980 Virago edition of *Monkey Grip* 'Junkie Jottings'. 'A diary of a storyless life. It just starts, it goes on, it just stops: no plot, no thickening, no knot, no dénouement. It could be read backwards.' The *Washington Post* was more thoughtful.[1] 'Garner is Australian, and it must be because her world view is significantly different from ours in the Northern Hemisphere that her methods of dealing with this material seem so refreshingly precise.' And the *New York Times Book Review*[2] found 'her fiction compelling . . . as if it is lit by an eerie slanted light . . .'

Even so, it was tough for any author gradually establishing a readership in that huge market. Helen once wrote to us from where she was reading to small houses at the New York City Library, '. . . *of course we are basically a non-event, we are from the void*, as far as most of these people are concerned. I develop a policy of expecting no one to turn up so that even seven people look like a big house.'

The US agents monitored how the authors performed and were quick with good advice. We were all learning on the run. Immediately Helen had given her first American interview to *Publishers Weekly*, before the publication of *Monkey Grip*, Ginger Barber contacted us and put it succinctly: 'Helen's quote about writing for Australians about Australia gave some people the wrong impression . . . the fact is, I agree with William Carlos Williams that the only "universal" is found in the "local" and I know that Helen didn't mean that she wanted us to be parochial. Her novels are for us all, even though she begins with Australians.'

The long haul around the world was essential so we could keep reiterating to agents and publishers, year after year, what it was exactly we were trying to do: selling Australian rights to new fiction and buying some American titles which might not be acquired by British publishers, or that we thought we could position better than they did in our market. Many of our authors didn't have agents, or, if they did, only in Australia. No one would place them overseas unless we did. This meant first of all building our credibility and maintaining connections with some of the powerful New York agents whose lists dovetailed with ours. New York was where we started each year.

They were mainly women, these agents that we dealt with – tough, funny, pragmatic women, like Ginger Barber who represented Virago's list, Lynn Nesbit, Liz Darhansoff, Charlotte Sheedy who had first tipped Diana off about the availability of some American fiction; Elaine Markson, who had been representing Jessica Anderson, Rodney Hall and John Hooker for several years and others such as Wendy

Weil, Elise Goodman and Heather Schroder, whom I got to know a little later. Each had impressive and individual lists which we pored over – and many had authors we knew we could publish more effectively in Australia than their current distribution arrangements through British publishers.

The agents pitched their authors at me with great pizzazz. And I learnt to pitch mine back, finding the words, the right spin, that would interest tough New Yorkers for whom Australia was a complete unknown, an offshore island of England. But we discovered we cared about many of the same things. We were doing all we could to find readers for books we knew deserved them, trying to make the world work for the authors we represented, and having a remarkably similar reading of the real shape of it.

They treated me as one of them and I was invited to hear their authors reading their work, to parties and to agents' meetings where publishers were being discussed, always critically. They gave me vivid glimpses of their New York lives. One lived in a Park Avenue apartment with a doorman and a rich husband and a view across the treetops in Central Park, her office across the hall as paper laden as my own. Another worked in a rabbit warren of a basement, filled with books and excellent coffee smells. Another was in a sparsely furnished elegant light-filled loft and she dressed to match. Some worked for large companies trading rights in all media; others worked from home in familiar chaos – book briefs, embroidered shawls, cats on every surface and, outside the door, the after-school sounds of Manhattan children. Another agent had just moved into a beautiful old apartment which was being renovated the day I first saw it by a gang of strong women painters in overalls, one of whom, I was eagerly told, was the daughter of an Australian war bride. I must meet her at once.

The world of rights sales and agenting is tiny, incestuous, funny and frank – to a point. Someone had reminded us from the first that the agents all knew each other and many were friends or former colleagues of publishers and agents we dealt with in London. It was essential not to put a foot wrong, to get it right from the start. Never be in town and not call; send what you say you'll send, and fast. One disastrous year I arrived to an ominous silence, no messages waiting for me at my cheap midtown hotel, my phone calls not returned for several days. Only after I flew out did I discover that a Melbourne mail strike meant that none of my letters had arrived before I did.

Selma Shapiro, a publicist who was regarded by many as the best in the business, had an office opposite the New York Public Library. Selma for several years had been retained by the Literature Board of the Australia Council, with the brief to promote Australian writing in America. There wasn't a lot of it around then. Selma rarely had authors with US publication dates and actual books to sell, and she did what she could for the steady stream of poets, novelists and academics who were passing through, but whose books were not available. Selma and her husband, Jim Silberman of Summit, then later of Little, Brown, who was also a storehouse of wise advice, must have endured dozens of meals with Australian writers with unrealistic expectations of an interview or a reading; but without books to promote in American stores there was a limit to what could be done.

By the early 1980s the New York agents were familiar with the argument coming from Canadian independents with strong lists, such as Louise Dennys, about the advantages of separating Canadian rights from the USA, so that Canadian publishers could bid separately for books they believed would do better with the individual attention that publishing, rather than distribution, could offer. The conglomerates, such as Penguin, Simon & Schuster, McGraw-Hill, and Random House, who saw their freedom to move stock across the border likely to be seriously curtailed, were resisting vigorously.

Our argument was a little different from Canada's. Australia was physically at least a completely separate market from Britain. We were on the other side of the world. Our history, though more recent, had real parallels with North America's, and our population was now even more diverse than most of the States. This was a picture of Australia that hadn't been given to them before, I was told again and again. That McPhee Gribble were interested in *buying* rights to American fiction and non-fiction as well as trying to sell our own list was again highly unusual. The agents were immediately interested and an avalanche of manuscripts and bookbriefs started arriving at the Fitzroy Post Office.

The publishers I saw regularly in New York were much more diffident. Many were surprisingly Anglophile, deeply protective of their London literary links, although they might also admit, or their agents would, that many of the authors they published were not being bought in London and that others were not selling in the kind of quantities they believed they deserved. Most publishers either produced for me the packages they would be selling at Frankfurt in October each year, books with titles like *High Level Wellness* and *How to be Married One Year from Today*, or they delivered kindly little lectures on the importance to mankind of the British connection.

The literary and scholarly independents treated us rather differently. Roger Straus at Farrar, Straus & Giroux, presiding over his wonderful shabby floors of book smells and braininess in Union Square, read our catalogue carefully, flattered me for a few minutes, then offered to sell us run-ons of 750 copies of their entire reprint programme – which would have turned McPhee Gribble overnight into a super-literary remainder house in the south seas. But his editors were enthusiastic and rights sales both ways gradually began to materialize. Ed Barber at W.W. Norton, a large independent scholarly press, knew at once what we were trying to do and gave us good advice. Griselda Ohannessian at New Directions on the nineteenth floor overlooking Staten Island, bought Carmel Bird on the spot because she loved her writing. Griselda, with her backlist of writers like Saroyan, Durrell and Miller, immediately understood what it was we were trying to build and a productive exchange began.

André Schiffrin, at the time one of a number of independent publishers in charge of his own list within a large publishing corporation, responded to books as ideas in the world rather than product. Schiffrin ran Pantheon within Random House US, and was interested in joint projects. Much of his list consisted of books that were rather too rarefied for us – a sumptuously decorated history of coffee, collections of European mythologies and folktales. But his major books were commissions of a kind no one else seemed to be doing – an oral history of World War II taken from Japanese soldiers and civilians was one which captured my imagination. Schiffrin would then build international print runs in English and in translation. He was the only publisher I met, apart from Carmen Callil, who remained immensely curious about the publishing possibilities in the region Australia inhabited. He visited McPhee Gribble in Fitzroy and I saw him often in New York and we began to plan together the commissioning of writers to do international books on the impact of missionaries, say, or an environmental history of the Pacific.

Gordon Lish was another with his own list at Random House, this time within Knopf. Lish was housed on the twenty-first floor of the Random House skyscraper in a tiny room with an antique desk and walls lined with his students' books and framed awards.

He produced under the Knopf umbrella a literary magazine, *The Quarterly*, which he assured me sold 40,000 copies an issue, and promoted the work of his 'stable'. Lish had been Raymond Carver's editor until Carver became uneasy with his interventions, and Harold Brodkey's, whose *Stories in an Almost Classical Mode*, which broke all records for late delivery, had just arrived when I first met him. Lish, who had a long and tart correspondence with Morris Lurie, who was now publishing with us, was almost a caricature of a literary editor, opinionated, deeply protective of his protégés, scathing about anyone not in his orbit. But he took me to lunch whenever I was in town and introduced me to Georges Borchardt, the agent who represented many of Lish's young authors – whose latest books he insisted I must add to my baggage and read on the plane.

Borchardt became one of the people in New York I would always try to see, calling on him at the end of my visits for his perspective on American publishing and writing, in his book-lined corner office on 57th and Lexington with its long views of both streets. His predictions about where international publishing was heading were astute – and seemed to me to be the face of the future for Australia also. It was Borchardt who reminded me that more than ninety per cent of Americans were graduating by the mid-eighties without studying American history, or any history of Western civilizations or foreign languages, and that only one in eighteen took any humanities subjects, compared with one in four taking business studies. Australia within a few years would not be much better. The gulf between literary and commercial publishing could only get wider as cultural literacy levels plummeted and the much more visual mass media took over.

American literary publishing, he said, was really a very small club, acutely conscious of catering for an intellectual élite. 'Roger Straus, Gordon Lish and I are freaks,' he told me, and certainly judging by the packaged, spin-doctored conservative product most of the conglomerates were pushing in offices where they may as well have been selling wallpaper, I could only agree with him. Borchardt, like so many of the agents I met, was critical of the commitments British publishers were making to literary authors and to 'big' books. He had not been to Australia – none of the agents or publishers I saw at that time had.

It was not until March 1988, when the Literature Board sponsored publishers and agents, that any of them made the journey and began to be able to visualize Australia as a market in its own right and a rather different one from Britain. The visit first took in Writers' Week in Adelaide then arranged meetings with publishers in Melbourne and Sydney. The guests included Ginger Barber; Ed Barber, Vice President of W.W. Norton; Paul Gottlieb, President of Harry N. Abrams; Michael Braziller of Persea Books; André Schiffrin of Pantheon Books and Stephen Rubin, Senior Vice President, Bantam Books, New York. Michael Klett, of Klett-Cotta in Stuttgart, and François Bourin from Editions François Bourin in

Paris also joined them as did Jim Silberman and publicist Selma Shapiro who had visited Australia before.

The Literature Board provided the publishers with
a business class airfare and A$2000 for a ten-day visit.
One of the main conditions of the invitation was that
'the invitee should not have visited Australia previously', explained Tom Shapcott, then Director of the
Literature Board, when he wrote to Australian publishers asking for their impressions of the scheme. In
replying, my irritation showed. 'Most of the publishers who came here struck me as not being short of a
quid whereas literary publishers and agents in this
country tend to be. There is also a danger of Australia
looking like a subsidised culture, even one which has
to pay people to come here. I got the distinct impression that some of the publishers were surprised to
have had their fares paid – particularly these days
when most of them know where Australia is and that
our writing is interesting.'[3]

It sometimes felt as if McPhee Gribble was trying
to drag Australia closer to the rest of the world by
sheer willpower. By 1989 we'd been spreading the
word about Australian writing for over a decade.

The first American novel we bought came not from
an agent or a publisher but from a suggestion made
by a young woman called Amy Rhodes, the sister of
an American friend in Australia, who worked in

Random House's marketing department. She mentioned over a drink one night that the book she'd
enjoyed most that year had been turned down by all
the leading British publishers. She sent me a copy to
read on the plane and here was a book I knew we
could sell in Australia – and which, remarkably,
Australians would not have been able to read unless a
British publisher had bought Commonwealth rights.
We published Wallace Stegner's *Crossing to Safety* a
few months later. 'A wise and good book,' said Tim
Winton in his coverline. 'I wish Stegner was one of
ours – and I wish this was one of mine.'

Stegner, too elderly to travel, did a number of telephone interviews for the Australian media. The book
was an immediate success and steadily reprinted. And
we had the perfect example of what we'd been talking about. Wallace Stegner, a major figure in
American literature, had published fourteen novels
and many works of non-fiction. He had founded the
Stanford writing programme which had had a pro-
found effect on contemporary American fiction. A
number of Australian writers had attended the course.
But because English publishers didn't rate Stegner
highly, his writing was almost unknown in Australia.

After Stegner we bought more – titles such as
David Bradley's *The Chaneysville Incident*, a powerful
black American historical saga which the British
agent, Bruce Hunter, acting for Wendy Weil in New
York, had not been able to sell in London; but he
knew enough about Australia to know that we could
make it work. Our publicist, Patty Brown, with a

small budget and the help of Bradley who came to Australia for publication, established the book well. We bought Australian rights to a Bharati Mukherjee novel and a collection of her stories, to Hugh Nissesen's *The Tree of Life* and to *Montgomery's Children* by Richard Perry. Don Anderson edited a collection of short stories from writers such as Raymond Carver, Donald Barthelme, Harold Brodkey, Susan Sontag and Bobbie Ann Mason called *Enchanted Apartments, Sad Motels* as a companion volume. Suddenly we had authors to meet in America, conversations to have about their next books, Australian authors to introduce them to, more manuscripts to read.

The search for available American titles we could publish well sometimes felt like the quest for the Holy Grail. I always went on to London after New York and the New York agent would, if I showed interest in a particular title, telephone the London agent who represented the author in the British Commonwealth, explaining that I might want to split off Australian rights and would call when I got to London. Most of the agents I dealt with had links with Abner Stein, an American agent who had lived in London for many years and who 'was more English than the English', I was warned.

Abner was always charming to me. Abner gave me a cup of coffee and an hour of his time as soon as I got in to London, then carefully, as if I might not understand, explained to me how publishing worked, and that he didn't want to upset his British publishing contacts, naturally. Of course he would send me some titles he knew I'd love. But I am fairly sure that Abner only sent me books he couldn't hope to sell.

Tessa Sayle, another British-based agent who also represented the lists of major US agents, and several Australian authors such as Thomas Keneally, and who became a friend, was rather more forthcoming but warned me that what I was trying to do was deeply unpopular, and more threatening than I realized. It would be best for authors, she agreed, but British sales figures, especially for fiction, were contracting, and losing an export market like Australia would not be tolerated.

One or two London agents did support us. Bruce Hunter at David Higham Agency had listened to me in the early eighties in his office with its leather chairs and cedar bookcases and portrait of the founder, and, somewhat to my astonishment, offered to help us. But Bruce, I discovered, was Canadian-born and had been to Australia several times. He had become Tim Winton's agent in the UK and had a perspective on the Australian market that was independent and forward-looking. Bruce was much more optimistic than I ever felt in London, especially after my visits to Abner, and adamant, he told me, that 'Imperialist publishing is over or will be soon. And the authors know it.' John le Carré had insisted on contracts for his most recent book which specified marketing and a separate advance in Australia from Hodder and, Bruce said, would have sought an Australian publisher if Hodder had not agreed. I left knowing Tim was in very good hands.

Deborah Rogers and Gill Coleridge, Anthea Morton-Saner and Mike Shaw at Curtis Brown were also sympathetic, agreeing that, ideally, Australia should be treated as a separate market, and were certainly prepared to represent authors who were separately published in Australia, but many other agents I saw regularly at that time were defensive and reluctant even to consider the benefits for the authors they represented. Why rock the boat by disturbing cosy traditional arrangements?

Working in London was debilitating. The energy I always felt sweep over me in New York, the range of possibilities I'd sensed there, would start leaking away almost as soon as I arrived at Heathrow. The publishers were offhand, many of them, given to cancelling appointments or not returning calls. The message, stated or otherwise, was that our authors, if they'd heard of them, would be far better off published out of London. We had nothing they wanted. Australian independent publishing was in the way.

Carmen Callil always rescued me and we'd have dinner and laugh and groan. Agents Tessa Sayle and Mary Clemmey helped sometimes too as did Virago's Ursula Owen as I got to know her – but none except Carmen understood the Australian market at that time or the complexities or depth of the tensions between the two countries. I leant heavily on friends who knew Australia and were as curious as I was about the differences – Anne Chisholm and Michael Davie and editor Helen Wire, a close friend since we'd first met on the beach in Greece.

To make matters worse I was suffering, by this time, from the certainty that my marriage to John was unravelling – and phone calls home were often miserable misunderstandings. After Penguin, John had spent a year or two running Thomas Nelson in Australia then for a time joined a mining company which exported rubies. We sailed as often as we could between the Bass Strait islands and in Port Phillip Bay. But having left Penguin insisting that *no one cave in*, John was wrestling with a black depression that grew worse and worse – disastrous for him and for all of us who cared about him. He designed and built a boat he named the *George Bass* – after the explorer best known for first circumnavigating Tasmania with Matthew Flinders in 1797–8 – and sailed her from Hobsons Bay to the Bay of Islands in the north island of New Zealand. Sailing for weeks on end, single-handed and mostly out of radio range, helped for a while.

I'd go in search of my old London whenever I could. The streets around Thurloe Square were so much more sparkling than they used to be and there was another Spanish couple in the basement of our building. The V&A was less dusty and rather better lit than I remembered, its skylights cleaned, its bounty more coherently housed, but the underlying assumptions and the omnipotence still gloriously on display. I'd find myself searching the faces of the merchants and naval men and their wives in the National Portrait Gallery for clues to Empire, which seemed to be seriously and richly represented only as far south as India. The portraits from the Australian colonial era were usually in drab colours with backgrounds undifferentiated or caricatured, signalling people marooned in a landscape few British settlers could see beauty in. I'd sit sometimes in St George's in Bloomsbury, a small and dark early eighteenth-century church with simple lines and a Corinthian portico which I'd always liked. Or just find a patch of grass and trees and watch the English clouds.

The great commercial heart, the centre of the publishing year, around the world, is the Frankfurt Book Fair, *Frankfurter Buchmesse*, a trade fair which has been in existence since 1948 and takes place in October. Here in an enormous multi-storey, many-halled supermarket, the world's publishing wares are laid out, by country, by language, by special interest groups, by media. There is one mighty *Halle* for the USA. The German publishers have another. *Grossbritannien* looms large with Ireland, Scotland, Wales under its wings, and most Australian publishers, their British links proudly on display, housed nearby. Frankfurt is a mighty map of the publishing world.

By the time I arrived at the Frankfurt Book Fair in October throughout the eighties, I would have been on the road for three weeks. The costs were considerable – round-the-world airfares, a few days in New York followed by, perhaps, visiting agents and publishers in

Canada or Paris, then a week in London before arriving in Frankfurt. Here I could take for granted that my bookings had gone wrong and I'd be in a room over the station or so far out of town I needed a weekly train pass. My suitcase was huge, the pack of sample books and catalogues was now full of other people's as well as our own and I lived in dread of losing the artwork that accompanied me everywhere.

Being an independent publisher at Frankfurt is tough wherever you come from. Being an Australian independent is about as tough as it gets. There is no one to help. Those who are subsidiaries of the big international groups have their bookings done for them. They work off their parent company's stands, and bask in their colleagues' gratitude when their on-the-spot commitment of several thousand copies of Australian support swings a deal their way. The publishers with head offices in London or New York are often beautifully and elaborately displayed with photographs of their reigning authors, personalized furnishings and deep carpets in colours coordinated to this year's promotions. There's even a glass-fronted bookcase or two. Editors, promotions and rights staff drive their displays south the weekend before the fair starts so everything is in place before the principals arrive.

The morning of day one opens with the CEOs in front of their stands like spruikers at a country fair. Others pad the aisles, henchmen in tow. In the eighties it was Paul Hamlyn, Peter Mayer, King of Penguin, Faber's Chairman Matthew Evans, Anthony Cheetham of Century, Bob Bernstein of Random

House US, Ian Chapman of Collins, who turned
heads. They'd stay for a short time, make their presence felt, then depart leaving their publishing
colleagues to do the deals. The grand old men and the
currently powerful were pointed out and gossip
would fly about impending mergers or takeovers and
those who were missing that year. But publishing has
a habit of recycling people and the same faces would
appear under different imprints year after year. The
senior women were often less conformist than the
men, who looked like executives of any corporation
in double-breasted suits and dark red ties. But baggy
tweed jackets and half-moon spectacles were signs of
high seriousness at Farrar, Straus, Cape, Faber,
Atlantic, and at the long established university presses.

The publishers with literary lists and the best
authors – Sonny Mehta of Knopf, Liz Calder of
Bloomsbury, Morgan Entrekin of Grove Atlantic,
Christopher MacLehose of Collins Harvill, Carmen
Callil of Chatto, Roger Straus of Farrar, Straus – the
star-agents, people like Andrew Wylie, and Caradoc
King of the 120-year-old London agency A.P. Watt,
created the real frissons. The competition was palp-
able. Some literary lists were becoming hot property.
The terms *coffee-table fiction* and *scholarly blockbuster* had
been invented. Advances for some authors were rising
way beyond the point that most publishers considered
could ever be earned back. Most agents worked out
of the Agents' Hall and the publishers queued to see
them, often doing their deals in earshot of each other.
Here I'd meet each year the network of sub-agents

we'd appointed to place our fiction in translation, agents such as Mary Kling in Paris, Sabine Orbach in Germany, Maydo Kooy in Holland, Eliane Benisti in Italy, Olé Licht in Scandinavia and William Miller of the English Agency in Japan.

Everyone worked spectacularly hard. Rights managers, usually rather frazzled-looking young women, wanted some guarantee that a ten-minute meeting with someone from the end of the earth would be worth their while. Appointments were every fifteen minutes if you had your own booth; if you were running from booth to booth, floor to floor, as did most independent Australians, Irish, Scots and Canadians, a great deal of time was spent standing on escalators waving at colleagues going the other way. There was much smoking and kissing and queuing for snacks and lunch stools in the bars and restaurants. DYNAMIC FOOD, the MILCH and things called FRANCETTES-BAGUETTES, filled with curry, ham, cheese or sausage, microwaved in their thousands, were ordered in bad German, and eaten all day.

Authors, unless they were once the President of the USA, or Martha Graham, have always been discouraged by their publishers from attending the Frankfurt Book Fair. A mighty literary figure like Rushdie or Sontag or Schama sometimes appears fleetingly – but anyone less secure in their international standing runs the risk of never writing again. This is the marketplace at work, a sea of a billion books and calculators and mobile phones and screens pumping out promos and video clips. It is not a place for readers or writers or for coherent thought.

What would an author make of the Bertelsmann party rumoured to be for 1500 people at eighty pounds a head in a salon of gigantic proportions with mirrored ceilings in the Hessehöff? Mountains of beautiful food surrounded by ice sculptures, pans of risotto as big as fishponds, trays of smoked salmon and horse-radish piled high above a fountain next to a harvest festival of fruit and flowers – presided over by dozens of chefs in tall hats. Waiters attend the clusters of well-upholstered publishing men, a large scattering of female publicists and editors and agents from Britain, Europe and North America. Whatever their nationality, the agents, usually women of a certain age, swathed in scarves and pashminas, look somehow alike. Everyone cruises the room seeking their own tribe or the hundred or so familiar faces in the publishing world that must be there somewhere. Germans talk to Germans, Dutch to Dutch, Australians to the English and as a last resort to each other. There are a few black faces – but only rarely from the old colonies. And the food tastes of nothing at all.

Being part of a conglomerate in the eighties also had its advantages when the pavilions closed at the end of each day. Then the independent publishers from the fringes, those who hadn't managed to ensure an invitation to the Bertelsmann party or to the McGraw-Hill or Penguin spread, or a friend to gate-crash with, congregated together, Fosters in hand, eventually confessing in the accents of Edinburgh, Dublin, Sydney and Toronto how few deals they'd actually managed to clinch. Australia and Canada and a few other 'emerging' publishing centres had national stands where the independent publishers pooled their resources to save money, displaying their new books, and sometimes some rather old ones, and giving away kangaroo tie-pins while keeping track of their appointments. But nothing really helped to ease the torture: the crucial thing was not to show you were feeling it.

Frankfurt is about buying and selling. It is how the book world really works. Australians took a few years to learn that we did better if we took books suitable for 'running on' with simple plate changes in different languages. Lifestyle, health, guide books, diet, popular biography and get-rich-quick schemes will do well provided they fit the mould, can be easily understood and summarized in a few words. Books with snappy titles like *Sex and Germs*, *The Nanny's Handbook*, *A Guide to Historic Medicine Bottles* will do even better.

The Fair is for maintaining contacts, showing strength, disguising weakness, displaying wares and doing deals. Most of the books are produced to fill slots in the market and to cater for a demand that is already there. There's not a lot of innovation and such as there is is usually dismissed as too risky. Disneyization and its imitators are everywhere. Animations, blow-up characters and giveaways are essential. Video clips bombard with the promise that here is next year's craze and record bestseller. Literature – which, unless the author is a brand name, still has to be read before it's bought – rarely flourishes at Frankfurt. The narrow aisles of scholarly publishing mostly look dull but worthy, with more and more energy and resources going into multi-media accompaniments. Many large university presses – Harvard, Yale, Stanford, Birmingham, Chicago, Oxford, Cambridge – nowadays compete for general books as well as maintaining some of their scholarly lists. The strength and variety of northern hemisphere English language publishing is indisputable.

Once I'd kept my appointments each year, seen our European agents, and sold what I could, the real interest for me lay in the non-English halls. It was like my guilty secret. I'd head there on my last day when Australian colleagues were still punching their calculators and queuing for the phones. The literary map of the world can be seen unfolding in the corridors of German, French, Italian, Scandinavian and South American publishers. The stands here are more modest and 'bookish' than those of their American and British counterparts and the displays of forthcoming titles and backlists miraculously still manage to retain their national character. Here can be seen the real strengths of English language literary lists – the rights sales of books that have penetrated throughout Europe and into South American markets from Knopf, Chatto, Cape, Faber, Farrar, Straus, Viking, Bloomsbury, Grove Atlantic, Harvill.

When we published Rod Jones' first novel, *Julia Paradise*, in 1986, we saw the international carpet roll out. *Julia Paradise*, a highly original work of fiction set in Shanghai and North Queensland in the 1920s, had, besides being very good indeed, several things going for it. It was about a psychoanalyst and a beautiful half-Chinese morphia addict. It was exotic and erotic. And it was short, which, since most novels grow by about a third in translation, possibly helped.

Even more important, it had two highly respected literary publishers talking it up as *a brilliant debut*. Rights had been sold to an ecstatic Tom Maschler at Jonathan Cape who, naturally enough, sought to visit the author in Queenscliff in Victoria on his next trip to Australia to suggest, I would imagine, that he transfer his allegiance to Cape and be properly published. When I later remarked to Maschler that the reverse might also happen sometimes too, that we could publish one of his favourite authors, Bruce Chatwin, say, in Australia rather better than his present arrangements, he was unamused. Jim Silberman at Summit, part of Simon & Schuster in New York, bought *Julia Paradise* for the US and translations into a dozen languages flowed from the enthusiasm of these men and these imprints.

By this time we had a network of sub-agents in place who sold the book in translation and the following year at Frankfurt I had the pleasure of seeing *Julia Paradise*, within a few months of British publication, in a dozen different editions on the European publishers' stands in French, Italian, German, the Scandinavian languages, Dutch, Portuguese, Spanish and Catalan. Placing other authors in translation became easier after that – but the key was always to ensure that British and American houses with the clout to convince the others purchased first.

Translations are usually left to publishers in the

northern hemisphere, despite the talented translators we have in our midst. Very occasionally books do flow from Australia in translation into the US and Europe without going through London first. But we are missing out on important books and essential bridge-building by not developing the capacity to publish in translation writing from our region to the north in particular.

McPhee Gribble had begun developing at this time a small list of writers in translation. There were new Chinese writers which China expert and translator Geremie Barmé had alerted us to, and a cultural revolution memoir, *Lost in the Crowd* by Yang Jiang, for which Farrar, Straus was interested in sharing print-runs with us. *A Foreign Wife* by Gillian Bouras was translated into Greek by Helen Nickas in Melbourne and eventually publication was arranged in Greece. Bouras was an Australian married to a Greek and living, with their two sons, in a Greek village. From the ambiguous position of a foreign wife, regarded as a curiosity, the migrant in their midst, she wrote of her life in her Greek family bringing up Greek sons. This was a book that sold widely in Australia, perhaps because it mirrored the position of 'foreigner' experienced by so many women in this country.

In 1986 we had admired the way new independent British publisher Bloomsbury 'went to the city'. With style, impeccable planning and high profile authors waiting in the wings, Bloomsbury positioned itself as 'literary mainstream', differentiated from other British publishers at the time – and raised nearly two million pounds for its launch. Later, Managing Director Nigel Newton remarked in an interview with the *Bookseller*[4]: 'Historically, many publishers have been founded on the proverbial shoestring and this may be one of the reasons behind the proliferation of houses that were in existence until recently, growing ripe to be taken over.'

Newton was talking about the British independents but he could just as well have been talking of us. Then, early in 1987, the Australian book trade press had been agog at the takeover of the British Group – Chatto, Cape and Bodley Head – by American Si Newhouse's US$7.5 billion Random House Group, which in the States owned Knopf, Ballantine, Modern Library, Vintage, Vogue as well as Random House itself. Simon Master moved from Pan in London to become CEO of the new group. Carmen Callil, now Chatto's Managing Director, was reported as saying, 'It's a heavenly agreement. I couldn't be happier about it,' and so it seemed. The enthusiasm around the new literary juggernaut was considerable, suddenly the possibilities seemed infinite for high quality publishing.

Sandy McGregor of Random House US was quoted as saying, 'Buying CCBH was one of the world's shortest negotiations.' The *Bookseller* in May that year interviewed Graham C. Greene, Chairman of the British Group. 'They wanted to build and not dismantle,' Greene said, delighted. 'The deal was building for the future.' And the Australian *Bookseller* with antipodean glee couldn't resist pointing out 'Now that the Chatto, Cape takeover is final that Group has admitted to debts of about A$7 mill.'

Carmen's address to the Society of Bookmen in 1994 explained some of the background to the merger seven years before: 'How to describe that antediluvian boys' club? . . . Selling to Random House saved them from bankruptcy. Increasing costs, author advances and the growing international market were the reasons we had to give up independence . . . There was a tragic waste of people at Chatto, Cape and Bodley Head. It doesn't matter how well-meaning the old manage-ment might have been, they were inadequate and inflicted real pain and suffering . . . Working for Random was a thousand times preferable to working for the old management. The first period was bliss.'

Meanwhile back in Australia, Diana and I had been hatching a plan to steadily expand the number of titles we published without Penguin's imprint on the books, and to do this as rapidly as we could. We were still managing on a working overdraft to pay our bills, to stay solvent, but the expansion would mean an injection of capital, which we'd never had.

The possibilities of seeking a quality list to sit beside our Australian publishing had been aired from time to time with publishing colleagues and friends in Australia and overseas. To do what we needed to do next, to secure the company's future and expand in the directions we wanted to go, an equity partner would be needed – preferably one, we hoped, from publishing or other media where the benefits would be seen to be mutual.

While Carmen Callil and I argued publicly, often privately we agreed that together we could develop a great list. We believed we would sell more copies of those titles we were committed to than the Chatto, Cape and Bodley Head Group could through their distribution arrangement in Australia at that time. Both of us firmly believed in companies being editorially led – where the books drive the marketing rather than the other way round. At this stage we were all thinking rather vaguely about joint imprints in Australia and marketing efforts for key titles – nothing too earth-shattering. And the next time I was in London Carmen arranged for the Group CEO, Simon Master, to take me to lunch 'to talk through the idea'.

After the usual exchange of compliments and industry gossip at the Groucho Club, I went through my paces. Master was politely encouraging but left me feeling uncomfortably aware that he regarded this as Carmen's baby not his. Such a deal would, of course, rock the CCBH distributor's boat in Australia. The advantages of more carefully pitched marketing and promotion which would have sold more books were of little interest.

After lunch, Master farewelled me at the door of the Groucho, murmuring that he was sure I wouldn't mind if he had to rush off – and I spent the next half-hour trying to hail a cab in the rain.

6

The Centre of the Universe

As an exotic site for artists and writers and serious travellers to visit, Australia could rarely compete with the rest of the world. Its meanings were not readily consumed and, once away from the cities, its ancient landscape required a response beyond words. By comparison with fabulous India – independent, political, intellectual, steeped in a shared tradition, its writers being heard all over the world, its relationship to England highly charged – Australia must have seemed bland and lacking in mystery. Africa, the Dark Continent, with its ancient kingdoms and wilderness, its tragic layers of exploitation and colonization, its political struggles, began on the other side of the Mediterranean, and there was South America and the Caribbean, whose great writers had already conquered us all. It is a fair guess that, for most British people, Australia in the eighties represented the affluent 'other', shallow and hedonistic. For a few there may have been some family stories,

residual memories or historical knowledge of a disturbing past to which they were irrevocably linked.
For Americans with any sense of Australia at all, we
were themselves in embryo, but far behind, still tied
to the Empire they had rejected two centuries earlier,
and straining from the bottom of the world to join
the club.

It was not until the eighties that Aboriginal
Australia and our convict past were transformed into
the stuff of international literature. When Robyn
Davidson's *Tracks*, an account of her journey across
Australia with camels, was first published in 1980 and
became a bestseller, it probably began the promotion
to a wide readership, including a literary one, of the
Australian desert landscape as a psychological as well
as a physical space of great subtlety. A generation of
writers, often visiting Australia for the first time as
guests of the Adelaide Festival's Writers' Week, began
to make pilgrimages of sorts to Ayers Rock and Alice
Springs.

The place was more elusive and the complexities
more difficult to negotiate than most visitors understood. When Werner Herzog made his film in 1984,
Where the Green Ants Dream, an uneasy combination
of environmental, anthropological and mystical concerns to classical music, he assembled a 'Central
Desert Tribe' near Coober Pedy in South Australia.
The cast was drawn from Arnhem Land many hundreds of miles to the north-east and the director
confused the Dreamings. Wandjuk Marika, the
statesman and elder from Yirrkala, later described the

outrage that Herzog caused among Aboriginal people. 'Because in that film the Dreaming is made up (that's a made up Dreaming, yes, it's a true story about the Green Ant Dreaming but from Oenpelli Dreaming . . . Green ants don't live in the desert; there's not trees, there's nothing trees, there's only plain country).'[1]

In 1982, English writer Bruce Chatwin arrived in Alice Springs seeking a way to write what he described as his 'quest in the desert'. Anthropologist Theodor Strehlow's *Songs of Central Australia* had been published in 1971, a record of 'ancient and traditional poems, intoned according to old and customary modes' collected from Aranda groups from 1932. Chatwin greatly admired Strehlow's work and was befriended by his widow. Strehlow had grown up at the Hermannsburg Mission where his father had been a Lutheran pastor, and where Albert Namatjira and his people had lived.

Chatwin visited twice and spent a total of nine weeks in the centre. In 1987 he published *The Songlines*, an account of what was in fact Chatwin's own dreamtime, his own imaginative response to Strehlow's work, his observations of the landscape and recollections of conversations he had with people who'd been working in the field for many years. *The Songlines* was an international success. It is still regarded by many readers as Chatwin's best work, and probably the definitive insight into the mind of that enigmatic traveller. Many in literary Australia also applauded his work, but it left a sour taste amongst those who knew something of the diversity and ambiguity of the field. Aboriginal Australia, they believed, had been plundered enough and now deserved only the most painstaking and tentative interpretation by anthropologists working side by side with Aboriginal people. In Alice Springs and far afield, Chatwin was considered someone who had breached secrets, extracted meanings he was not entitled to repeat from long conversations with Aboriginal leaders such as Pat Dodson, and reworked what he found. His response to subtle and secret information was seen by some as appropriation and distortion.

Chatwin filtered what he found through his own imagination to fit his own needs and left some people feeling betrayed and manipulated or concerned on behalf of others. Had Chatwin been an Australian writer, reviewers would very likely have exposed the flaws and consigned the book quietly to the remainder tables. Had Chatwin been writing about Zimbabwe or Patagonia, as he did in an earlier book, his accuracy and ethics would have gone unremarked in Australia. As it was, the idea of Australia being crisscrossed by 'songlines' became embedded in popular understanding – but they are an Englishman's literary construct, not the authentic and sacred Aboriginal meanings which are almost impossible to convey in words.

In Australia much was going on. There was the revelation for many people of Aboriginal art, a deeper sympathy with Aboriginal spirituality from the 1970s and an understanding which began with people working in the field, that Aboriginal culture was infinitely complex. Research in anthropology, ethnography, prehistory, the geological and environmental sciences was identifying much that was unique.

The desert landscape had been a source of replenishment and imagery for artists since the 1950s and earlier. Sidney Nolan, Margaret Preston, Russell Drysdale, Fred Williams, John Olsen, Jan Senbergs and many others made excursions outback sometimes accompanied by writers and film makers. John Wolseley, a painter who came to Australia from England in the early 1970s, was engaged by the strangeness and ancientness of where he found himself. He stayed to work on his vast meditations on Gondwanaland and its primordial links with South America and the Asian archipelago, seeing something resembling 'deep time' or 'deep past' in his layered archaelologies.

Until the 1970s when there was a considerable increase in the amount of specialized research, there were great gaps in our knowledge and understanding of our own prehistory and of Aboriginal Australia. There were unexamined or inadequate records of missions and government agencies. There was now a general acceptance in Australia that fieldwork needed to be considerably more painstaking and cooperative, both across disciplines, and between experts and communities, than ever before. The debates about the control of the archaeological record, between science and the Aboriginal custodians, were fundamental to

an appreciation of the cultural complexities and sensitivities that had to be negotiated. The layers of shame
and dispossession could no longer be ignored by
white Australians now hoping to work collaboratively
with Aboriginal people.

It was not acceptable nor particularly interesting
for Aboriginal stories to be simply retold in gram-
matical English or paraphrased by non-Aboriginal
writers then mediated through publishing processes
without consideration. Protocols for whitefella publication were being established through experience
and with advice from the Aboriginal Arts Board
which had been established in 1973 under Whitlam.
Books were being published in Australia from the
seventies which had grown out of the new radical
sensibilities, the land rights movement, and the testi-
monial and autobiographical writing of Aboriginal
people. Charles Perkins' *A Bastard Like Me* and Kevin
Gilbert's *Living Black* had been published by 1977 and
during the next decade a number of accounts by
Aboriginal writers such as Sally Morgan's *My Place*,
Ruby Langford Ginibi's *Don't Take Your Love to Town*
told the stories of their lives.

But we may well have been the only publishers in
1983 prepared to take on Elsie Roughsey's *An
Aboriginal Mother Tells of the Old and the New*. The
handwritten manuscript was brought to us by two
researchers from the Aboriginal Data Archive at the
University of Queensland. It had survived a cyclone
on Mornington Island, passing through the hands of
several custodians until it reached Paul Memmott and

Robyn Horsman. Part autobiography, part testament, part philosophical statement, it was one of the few accounts of tribal and mission life to survive, largely in its original form.

Elsie Roughsey had been born in 1923, a member of the Lardil tribe from Mornington Island, or Goonana, in the southern Gulf of Carpentaria. Her parents called her Labumore after the fruit of a native plant. In 1972 she sat down to write the story of her life for her own people and for those she described as being 'in the outside part of the world', from the time of her birth to tribal parents, and spanning the arrival of white missionaries to the present. 'When I was born, my mother and her friends made a rough circle of wind break for my arrival, so my mother could be kept warm and find her baby without harm.'[2]

From the age of eight, Labumore, called Elsie, was raised in a mission dormitory which aimed to educate and condition Aboriginal children in European ways. Her brothers and sisters, unbeknown to her, were in the same mission, working in the same gardens, attending classes, carrying water in kerosene tins for washing.

> To get up early in the morning, the missionary lady or one of her children comes with the keys and opens the padlock, and we all rush out of the dormitory, just to be free, free as Summer's bird . . . then wash our faces, grab a stick and bucket and go down to the well to fill a large tank for the day's drink, for all the boys and girls and the Adults who had a job to do in the mission, while the boys go out to bush

and bring in wood to cook all our meals. We do
these jobs every morning before we have our breakfast. We never sit around.[3]

On Sundays their parents would walk into the mission to join in the church service. During the early
years of the war Elsie and the other mission children
were sent back to live in the bush with their families
– a difficult transition – until the missionaries
returned in 1946. She describes her work in the
community as a nursing assistant and teacher aide,
raising her family in the 'old and new ways', and her
attempts to revive Aboriginal culture on Mornington
Island. Her husband Dick Roughsey became the first
Chairman of the Aboriginal Arts Board.

Nothing was incompatible for Elsie in the two systems of belief, her people's stories intermingle with
Bible stories, but there was much to mourn in the
destruction of the Lardil culture and the cruelties her
people experienced. 'Finally . . . crept in the white
man, with all its different hard life, with the laws of
Government, that drove away all our good ways of
living. I wondered much about this.'[4]

Having typed the original to preserve as much as
possible the work's authenticity, Elsie's syntax, and
the strong links her writing had with traditional oral
story-telling, the academic editors worked closely
with her to produce a final manuscript. The text was
divided into paragraphs and chapters, some spellings
and tenses were standardized and additional punctuation was introduced in order to 'make reading easier'.

The transition from manuscript to published work raised a number of questions which had to be negotiated. We shared the concern to preserve and represent the originality of Elsie's voice, but, since publication as a book is not a snapshot of a manuscript, some compromises were suggested. 'The act of typesetting does remove the written form to a large extent. The pages [must] not look as if they are full of typesetting mistakes or that the book has been published less "professionally" than other books,' we wrote to the editors. Typesetting and text design which applied some rules of consistency had to be a consideration, both to attract readers to begin with, and then to encourage them to read on. The tension was a familiar one, fundamental to quality publishing and, to me, endlessly interesting. How, without compromising the work, can readers be enticed in large enough numbers to make publication possible?

Diane Bell's *Daughters of the Dreaming*, a much-debated ethnographic study of Walpiri women's lives, was the result of long research in the field. Bell, an anthropologist, had lived with her children at Warrabri, a government settlement located 375 kilometres north of Alice Springs in the Central Desert. She argued that women's ritual and knowledge of the Dreaming Law, *jukurpa*, so different from men's, was of equal status and interlinked with it, before the loss of the land and the destruction of social structures wrought by whites. Diane Bell then worked closely with her editor and designer to produce a book which read clearly, without weakening its scholarly and theoretical framework, and still captured a good deal of the warmth and trust that underpinned her work. A group of Walpiri women came shyly into the office one day with Diane on their first visit south and we showed them the cover proofs and the photographs we wished to use. Protocols about not reproducing images or naming people who had recently died were regularly abused and there was much anxiety in Aboriginal communities as a result. The stories of visiting anthropologists and photographers who failed to honour their promises to send copies of photographs or published accounts were legion – especially as interest in Aboriginal Australians was growing internationally.

Soon after this we published *Growing Up the Country* by Phillip Toyne and Dan Vachon, an account of the struggle of the Pitjantjatjara people for their traditional land in a vast area around and including Ayers Rock. After years of legal negotiation and demonstration, in a ceremony which took place on 25 August 1984 before a huge gathering of Pitjantjatjara and supporters, the Rock was renamed Uluru, and the Pitjantjatjara people regained their land. Yami Lester, blinded as a boy in the Maralinga atomic tests in north-central South Australia, wrote a moving prologue to the book. Maralinga had been selected by the British and Australian governments for a series of explosions between September 1956 and 1958 despite the Aboriginal communities living in the vicinity, and many people had been permanently damaged. Now an old man, Yami described how he 'had to run away from the policemen in order to stay with my family. I saw my half-caste relations taken away and sent down to Adelaide to be educated in European ways, and it was a sad time for us.'[5]

Next we produced the first account in book form of the culture of the Kulin people of Port Phillip who had once inhabited the lands that lie beneath the city of Melbourne, where they met for ceremonies and food gathering and set their fishtraps along the river Yarra. There was a growing awareness of Aboriginal sites and sacred places and an interest in the original landscape covered by the urban environment and the farmland surrounding Melbourne. With Gary Presland from the Victorian Archaeological Survey, we set out to produce a book that reconstructed as best we could through archaeological and historical sources the period just before and after the destruction of Aboriginal culture and landscape.

> On 28 March 1839, when the settlement was less than five years old, between four and five hundred Aborigines gathered in a camp in what is now the Botanic Gardens. They had come from many directions to make up a welcoming party for the newly arrived Chief Protector of Aborigines, George Augustus Robinson.[6]

Experts in their field who can write well are rare – and by the eighties universities were no longer places where writing time was readily available. *Efficiency, effectiveness, participation* and *equity* were the buzz words of the Hawke government – and were used to justify endless restructuring and the creation of juggernaut institutions. Academic authors seemed to us to be more embattled, administratively overloaded, yet more dependent than ever before on publication for promotion.

We read lots of theses and research papers hoping to find a book shimmering there beneath the layers of methodology and scholarly apparatus, or concealed in the language of experts. Often their authors were attracted to the idea of writing for a general readership, but only rarely could they face the amount of rewriting required. Academic writing did gradually become more adventurous, topics less conventional, but anxiety seemed to mount about the effects of 'popularizing', as if non-scholarly publishing inevitably led to the work being compromised to satisfy the demands of a wide audience.

Others found that they could work with their editors to produce books that had long lives and were still academically respectable. This kind of publishing absorbed a good deal of editorial time as themes were developed, and went through several drafts, but the books were better for the talk around them, and many reprinted steadily – the ideas sometimes seeming to flow out like ripples in a pond. 'The books talk to each other,' was how one of the editors put it trying to explain the echoes and resonances we were sometimes aware of.

Lucy Frost's *No Place for a Nervous Lady* was a collection of unpublished letters and diaries from women in nineteenth-century Australia, women such as Annie Baxter whose writings had sustained her through a miserable marriage to a military man and failed farmer, and who wrote to her friend after being bled with a penknife, 'Oh! ye nervous ladies, never come to the bush!' *No Place for a Nervous Lady* repaid the many weeks of effort put into it by our editors and Lucy Frost as she painstakingly interpreted and annotated the women's words.

Consideration of landscape and our place in it was always a strong strand in Australian writing and it became stronger as environmental issues came to the fore. John Blay's *Part of the Scenery*, an account of his solitary trek deep into the almost impenetrable Back Country near the south coast of NSW and his meditation on the bush, was published in 1984, followed by Chester Eagle's *Mapping the Paddocks* and *House of Trees*, two fine studies of rural life and the countryside. Barney Roberts brought us his memoir of childhood, *Where's Morning Gone?*, written from a point of great stillness. Apart from the five years spent as a prisoner of war in Germany from 1940–45, he had lived all his life in Flowerdale, in Northern Tasmania, as a farmer and writer. *Where's Morning Gone?* had a story-teller's rhythms and a wisdom about it found occasionally in the memoirs of people whose lives have been shaped by living in one place for a long time. But only Barney sent his editor pressed boronia from his garden.

The new generation of academic historians, such as Stuart McIntyre, Marilyn Lake, Ann Curthoys, Jenny Lee, Verity Burgmann and Pat Grimshaw, concerned with the new curricula and the declining numbers of students taking history subjects at senior school level, sometimes discussed their ideas with us at an early stage. Lee and Burgmann edited *The People's History of Australia*, a massive project in four volumes bringing together more than seventy historians, who reconsidered Australian history from perspectives usually ignored or sidelined – the kitchen, the factory floor, the school-room, the small farms, the dispossessed Aboriginal population. Michael Cathcart worked closely with his editor to adapt a thesis which was also a great story – about Australia's secret army intrigue of 1931, when groups of armed men began forming vigilante organizations to combat the threat of socialism. *Defending the National Tuckshop* and Belinda Probert's *Working Life*, a study of the meaning of work, were books that had long lives – at least partly because their authors were determined from the outset to write for more than their colleagues.

The Grand Old Men of Australian history – Manning Clark, Geoffrey Serle and Geoffrey Blainey and others – with their reputations made and their relationships firmly in place with their publishers of long-standing, befriended us and sometimes sought our advice. These were usually matters of sales or royalty statements from their university presses, or concerns on behalf of younger colleagues whose work they were promoting. But they all were chafing at the unwillingness of their publishers to allow inexpensive paperback editions of their books onto the market. Geoffrey Serle knew his biography of John Monash and his general histories had audiences beyond the scholarly but his publishers refused to sub-contract to other publishers with stronger distribution. Manning Clark sometimes spoke about *giving you a book one day* but also, a little regretfully, perhaps, about the *succès d'estime* that went with a university press. Our shabby premises weren't really in the race. We would read their contracts, advise firm action on the grounds that, without effective distribution, and with booklists sporting headings in Latin, the general market could never really be available to them. We were listened to courteously, but nothing changed.

Geoffrey Blainey, on the other hand, was unique amongst his colleagues for always seeking a wide readership through his publishers, Macmillan, and taking most seriously his non-expert readers. He too called in to our offices occasionally – with the slight hint hovering about him that we might find ourselves offered a new *Triumph of the Nomads* or a *Tyranny of Distance*. One day, in 1984, quite soon after his now notorious Warrnambool speech, Blainey arrived for a coffee and said that he proposed to give us a book. Intentionally or not, the speech had first set the hares running by suggesting that current policies of multiculturalism were causing racial tensions, that Asian immigration to Australia was too far in advance of popular opinion and should be slowed. The book, which might have led to some interesting editorial discussions, didn't eventuate for us, but his daughter Anna joined us as a part-time receptionist and occasional researcher for the next year or so.

Blainey's ability was to communicate far beyond his colleagues and capture the popular imagination with practical details about how the world had worked in the past – how clocks were set in country towns, what the distance between places actually meant. He was matched only by Robert Hughes whose eloquent account of 'the first Gulag' – the British penal colonies in New South Wales and Van Diemen's Land – *The Fatal Shore*, was published in 1987, and written for a non-expert readership around the world. Writing from America, Hughes was able to sidestep the kind of debates that often paralyse writers closer to home, keeping them looking over their shoulders, watching their backs. The intent of the legislators and the extent and consequences of the penal system under which modern Australia was founded had been regularly reassessed and reinterpreted by Australian scholars. When Hughes' book landed, some academics saw their territory encroached upon, many were critical of his colourful language and his interpretation of the evidence. Others saw the book as a beat-up – created by a large advance, a massive marketing budget and an international sales pitch. But Hughes had done the research, knew how to write for many audiences – and, possibly, it had taken an expatriate to see the 'big' story beneath the facts.

An illustrated children's history of Australia bringing together the new research and fieldwork of the last fifteen years was badly needed but general histories were out of fashion. Early in 1984 historian Don Watson had published *Caledonia Australis*, a quirky revisionist study of the pastoral frontier in Gippsland, Victoria. It included a chilling account of the treatment of Aboriginal inhabitants by (mainly Scottish) settlers. Watson was also writing political satire for Max Gillies' stage and television shows. An historian with the ability to write entertainingly seemed ideal for our project. We wanted a book that told stories and engaged young readers with issues in Australian history which resounded in the present. Don was convinced and in concert with our designer, illustrators and researchers, *The Story of Australia* was produced in less than a year.

We began the story with the ancient fossil record of 500 million years ago and the archaeological discoveries of recent years that had confirmed earlier evidence that Australian Aborigines had come from the north at least 50,000 years ago. But full weight was also given to Aboriginal Dreamtime stories which place creation within Australia rather than offshore. There were plenty of heroes and heroines, chronologies and stories of ordinary people from all over the world who had made their lives here. *Captain Cook did not discover Australia, Who Owns the Past? The Massacre at Myall Creek, Milking Cows and Listening to Tarzan, A House, a Holden and a Hills Hoist, The Right to the Land* were some of the page headings. We ended the book with what seemed to us a revealing and poignant fact: *There are now more hairdressers than steelworkers in Australia.*

On p. 148 of the first edition of *The Story of Australia* are two black-and-white photos taken during the Great Depression. Don's father, aged in his early twenties, stands grinning proudly by a cartload of dead rabbits on a country road. My father at the same age, 'lucky to have a job' and in an ill-fitting suit, stands behind his first boss, a trapped look on his face.

I was on shaky ground when Don and I decided to live together. The office had an unwritten rule that publishing and love affairs with authors didn't go together. They made for poor editorial judgement, the risk of over-enthusiasm or, worse, an orphaned book if the going got rough. But *The Story of Australia* emerged unscathed and went into a number of editions. And we lived happily ever after.

One day in the mid-eighties, political psychologist Graham Little arrived with the intention of persuading us to publish a collection of the last essays of the late Professor Alan Davies which his colleagues wanted to bring out in his honour. Commemorative volumes we usually turned down because the print-runs were too small and the readership too restricted. But Graham persuaded us that Davies' teachings, in which psychoanalytical ideas were brought to bear on the study of politics and power, had been ground-breaking. In a culture that tended to shy away from

the ideas of Freud, and a conservative academic environment, Alan Davies had taught Graham Little,
Judith Brett and others, several of whom went on to
apply psychological readings of politics and Australian
society for a wide public through their newspaper
columns and commentaries. We published *The
Human Element* and Graham's next book, *Speaking for
Myself*, and he became a good friend and part of the
life of the office.

Graham once said that McPhee Gribble reminded
him of the Elves and the Shoemaker. He would drop
in some chapters and, the next day, there they would
be in their proper place, assembled and edited and
ready to go to the typesetter, as if by magic. He
would sometimes arrive and stand there watching us
with great curiosity as, all around him, we were
working with books. It wasn't magic, it was simply a
way of doing things which allowed a small group of
people with skills to become involved in the books as
they evolved, prepared to consider the parts as well as
the whole. But I like to imagine how it must have
looked through his eyes.

We had become aware in the early eighties, along with
everyone else Brian Matthews knew, and well before he
had a manuscript he was willing to show for it, that he
was struggling to write a book about Louisa Lawson. It
was a fairly foolhardy act to try to write 'about Henry

Lawson's mother', with all the embedded literary folklore and biography that surrounds them both. Louisa Lawson's life had left only archival remnants. There are huge gaps in the story of the Mother of the Suffrage, mother of Henry and Gertrude and Charles, founder and editor of the *Dawn*, the newspaper which set out in the 1890s to revolutionize women's lives, to fit them to become the leaders of the new order. Matthews found himself having to invent a narrative voice and a methodology; and, more difficult still, a device that would let him think aloud about the difficulties he faced – the dearth of material at key points in Louisa Lawson's life, and his need to reconcile differing versions of events.

As the manuscript gradually emerged, editorial discussions at first revolved around the kind of device that would set Brian, the biographer, free, and a structure for the material so that the reader did not go away. *Louisa* was, for several years, very much part of the office, sometimes at the centre of its gossip, its editorial discussions, in our trying to find the right design solutions to a many-layered work with no apparent precedents. The author had different editors at different stages as the manuscript evolved: first me, then Joan Grant and lastly Jane Arms who not only worked with Brian to bring the manuscript to its final state of clear resolution, but eventually married him. But it was not until Brian created a character called the Biographer, whose *alter ego,* Owen Stevens, illuminated what he was up to in ways a diary or letters never could, that the real breakthrough occurred. The

Biographer was now free to roam between fact and fiction, theatre and poetry, discontinuities and story while holding the reader in the palm of his hand.[7]

Louisa was written at a time when all publishers were seeing a lot of what purported to be postmodern writing: some, especially fiction, thinly veiled exercises, as if a template had been taken to an idea and the work arranged to fit; some works of intellect rather than imagination but with little purchase on history or experience. But the originality of *Louisa* still shines through. The multiple voices and mirrors reveal Louisa Lawson in ways a more conventional biographer or historian could not. Re-reading the book and the files recently reminded me that *Louisa* was originally on offer simultaneously to a university press and to McPhee Gribble. I remember our delight – which may have caused the story to become a little exaggerated – when the press decided to turn the book down because it was 'unconventional' and because one of the publisher's readers 'wondered what the author would make of the book in five years' time'. I don't know the answer to that but I do know that the publication of *Louisa* in 1987 probably marked a turning point in Australian biographical writing.

It wasn't all plain sailing, of course. We were building a list we were proud of, but we were still always seeking big projects that would boost the cash flow and help pay the wages bill. These were sometimes a mixed blessing – good ideas at the time and torment in the making.

The year before the 1988 Bicentennial, Australian publishers were commissioned to produce so-called 'Landmark' publications and we were awarded two of them, for women and for children, predictably. The first became *Generations*, a collaboration between anthropologist Diane Bell and photographer Ponch Hawkes, where grandmothers, mothers and daughters from all over Australia spoke of the way the significant objects in their lives had been passed on from hand to hand, generation to generation.

The second of the Landmark commissions nearly sank us. This was a children's encyclopedia, a kind of giant *Practical Puffin*, a history and geography book with projects, an introduction to politics, civics, land rights – everything an Australian child ought to have in their head, according to us, in 1988. We were imagining the impossible – or something that only an online virtual museum could provide. Joan Grant was persuaded away from academia to coordinate and edit the book and the task of researching, writing and illustrating the *Australopedia*, as we rather clumsily named it, permeated the whole office. A postcard from Robyn Annear when I was overseas in 1987 captured the worst time as the deadline approached: 'The *Australopedia* seems to hang over us like some great, looming, leaden thing – it's hard to associate it with something fun and bursting with colour and movement that we hope it will emerge as . . . Everyone seems to teeter on the brink of beserkness and the mere mention of the word *Australopedia* jerks us a fraction closer to the pit . . .'[8]

Our little Macintosh was working overtime upstairs with the editors and by now the PC we had recently acquired was fully occupied day and night producing spreadsheets and business plans. Joan Grant and those who were seconded to help her waded through vast amounts of newsprint and reference material, briefed illustrators, solicited diagrams and charts from experts who were often not at all good at communicating with children. Joan did a remarkable job considering the scope of the book and the difficulty of organizing such a range of material with extremely limited technology and staff resources. Somehow, in spite of it all, we succeeded in producing a book that won awards and was close enough to our original grand idea.

Anyone with half an eye on Australian writing in the early eighties was aware of Tim Winton, the talented young West Australian writer who, unlike most of his contemporaries, was taking on the large themes like those of Melville, White and Hemingway. 'It's as if Winton has impatiently bypassed the adolescent revolt stage, and gone straight for the big questions,' Helen Garner wrote when she reviewed *An Open*

Swimmer, Tim Winton's first novel, which Allen & Unwin published in 1982. Tim Winton was just twenty and had won the Vogel Award for a new writer.

> It had been a long fight between Jerra Nilsam and the fish. He pressed the flat end of the oar against its brow. Globes of moisture clustered on its flanks. His father grinned in the stern. The engine was chuckling. Water parted like an incision behind. The fish grunted. His father said it was a turrum. The long fan of tail slapped the gunwale, the gills were pumping, and blood globbed the bottom of the boat.[9]

These were the first words I ever read of Tim Winton's and re-reading this opening paragraph now nearly twenty years and more than fifteen Winton books later, I can see how it resonates with the books and characters that followed – with Fish Lamb in *Cloudstreet*, with Lockie Leonard, with Ort Flack and his father in *That Eye, the Sky*, and with Scully in *The Riders*. The voice was distinctive, as were the images of the coast where Tim had lived all his life, and of the people he'd grown up with and heard about in stories brought home by his policeman father.

We were pleased but not too surprised when literary agent Caroline Lurie rang one morning and asked if we'd like to talk about Tim Winton, the youngest-ever recipient of the Miles Franklin Award for his second novel, *Shallows*. What did surprise us was that Tim's initial publishers were willing to let him go.

Apparently he'd wanted to publish a collection of stories next – and Allen & Unwin 'didn't want him to', Caroline Lurie said. Nor, probably, would most other publishers at that time. Received publishing wisdom maintained that collections of Australian short stories didn't sell and that authors should be firmly discouraged from producing them. We had published several collections, which had been well received – Barry Hill's *A Rim of Blue* and *Headlocks* and Beverley Farmer's *Milk* and *Home Time*. So we knew there was a readership out there if the stories were strong enough, and Tim Winton's audience was growing.[10]

For McPhee Gribble, this was the beginning of a ten-year relationship with Tim Winton, although he lived as far from Fitzroy as it was possible to be, beside a surf beach on the other side of the continent, and was only able to visit the office once a year or so. He became a friend of us all and, for me, there was the huge satisfaction of being Tim's editor as his international reputation grew steadily and as an unprecedented number of translations and editions of his backlist were sold overseas.

Tim's writing was like no one else's from the start and carved out for me its own space in my head. He has always used rhythm to great effect, and short sentences and single words like blows. In the first paragraph of his first book he invents language like 'globbed'. And somehow you trust him wherever he takes you – into natural lore, the workings of boats and the mysteries of fish. There's a loving regard for the web of it all.

In the first year our letters were careful exchanges.

We had not met so he was unsure and rightly nervous of editorial advice, and we were tentative, not knowing yet how to anticipate his reaction to suggestions about the selection of stories and the style of cover designs. Western Australia was a long way off and we didn't ring each other often. We were all poor – his publishers always looking for ways for one of us to visit him, or for invitations that would include a plane fare for 'the young Perth writer who is off and running', as the *West Australian* liked to describe him. We were acutely conscious that Tim and his wife Denise were battling on our small advances and six-monthly royalty cheques as his list of books grew.

From the dates alone, it would appear to have grown effortlessly. From 1984 and for the next ten years a manuscript a year was delivered to us. Tim's professionalism was striking. He would rework painstakingly, usually in his clear handwriting. We published *Scission* in 1985 quickly followed by *That Eye, the Sky* which was launched by Helen Garner at Writers' Week in Adelaide. Here we saw the first signs of the guru status some people wanted to confer on him. Crowds of young people mobbed his signings and there were others who followed him everywhere. Tim's Christianity was always a powerful undercurrent to his writing, and central to *That Eye, the Sky*, and was no doubt part of the aura some people wanted to see around him, of a young spiritual leader, which he did not seek out or enjoy.

Elizabeth Jolley wrote to us when *That Eye, the Sky* was published, 'I am glad Tim has written it for I think it is a book which can do nothing but good in this world of books of ours . . .'[11] Then came another collection of stories, *A Minimum of Two*, and the first of his books for children, a picture book titled *Jesse* after his first-born son. Tim's work was highly praised, his status as a 'wunderkind' was constantly referred to and he was much in demand. Overseas publishers began to sit up and take notice. Soon he was *wrestling with the Poms*, as we called it. Letters came from editors in British publishing houses and agents interested in acquiring rights. Sometimes they made suggestions. 'The surfing element we feel is fine. Indeed, it adds quite a lively visual edge to the story . . . but I think we may have just a bit of difficulty with specifically Australian slang terms such as "dag" and "spack" or a more Australian vocabulary, such as "cacking" (which had us a bit puzzled).'

This advice, if heeded, would have watered down everything that had made them single out Tim's work in the first place.

By the mid-eighties, Australian writing and all the critical, promotional and festival apparatus that went with it was firmly established. Literary awards began to proliferate. State premiers were persuaded to allocate funds for prizes for writers in various genre and media. In 1975 there were three or four major literary awards; by 1986 there were twenty-five.

Publishers who, ten years earlier, were warning us to avoid writers of fiction who were all *difficult and demanding and didn't sell*, were establishing fiction lists of their own. The conglomerates justified their investment on the basis that Australian fiction was now sought after, bookshops liked having local authors around and would better support UK and US titles as a result.

As competition increased, the marketing and promotion of authors everywhere became more sophisticated. The colour supplements and magazines discovered writers' profiles and so occasionally did television. Public personas were marketable and soon seemed an important ingredient in a work's success. Some authors understandably resisted. Beverley Farmer, when awarded the New South Wales Premier's Prize for Fiction in 1984, for *Milk*, responded by saying only that 'Writing is not a performing art' and sitting down again to loud applause. One or two authors made their non-availability to the media a marketing ploy. Others were more than happy to treat the new interest as a way of communicating with readers, and writers' panels and readings proliferated.

Writers reading their work to a live audience became, by the mid-eighties, particularly popular in Australia and Canada, slower to spread widely in the UK and US, perhaps as a result of the success of Adelaide Writers' Week and of Canada's Harbourfront Writers' Festival. The salon-like Mietta's in Melbourne and the Harold Park Hotel in Sydney became for a while hubs of literary life in their cities, attracting audiences of all ages to hear new and established writers reading their work. A generation of television may have created a hunger for unmediated experience of writers and their words, and the increase in interest which flowed on into book sales.

The mid-eighties was also the period when we began to see some of the results of the expansion of the creative writing classes into universities. There were novels written as MAs, collections of stories written as class exercises, taught, usually, in English departments with occasional sessions from established writers describing the publishing experience or sharing thoughts about adjectives or structure. That universities were now discussing creative processes and encouraging them in their students was valuable. When conducted by the best writers available and combined with an analysis of a range of fine writing, much good could come from the courses. Wallace Stegner had pioneered the great creative writing classes at Stanford – but most American and Australian courses fell short of these and only rarely produced writing, in class conditions, that seemed to us to be publishable. Some did find publishers and probably contributed to what the media liked to call the *creative outpouring* from first-time novelists. The rush to publish and the desire to build fiction lists would mean a lot of failures – critically and commercially. And by the end of the eighties, publishers would have grown disenchanted with books that failed to sell out first print-runs and start to back away from properly supported fiction publishing.

Right from the start we published first novels. A few were from writers we never heard from again and I wonder occasionally still if they are struggling somewhere or have found no need to continue. Many others went on to write several books, some ranging across the rather artificial fiction–non-fiction divide, others producing short stories and novels at fairly regular intervals.

Writing books must be the most isolated of the arts. The act of writing is a private one with nothing between the writer and the page or screen. Words which were working well one day can unravel the next. The imagined critics are rarely benign. Even after a decision has been taken to publish, the editor is often the first person to read the work in depth, and respond on behalf of future readers. Much can depend on that first response. A relationship of trust – that their words are in good hands – is the best starting point, and way through, when things go wrong as they almost always will at some point in the months before publication. Most publishers have not submitted themselves to their own processes or written even ten thousand words of sustained prose. Most authors are not good at knowing the kind of help they need – or at asking for it.

The writing and editing time is always intense and potentially fraught with misunderstandings and sensitivities. Our way of working evolved as we grew more experienced, saw much writing at an early stage and began to understand something of the anxieties and uncertainties that plague most authors.

We made lots of mistakes like all publishers do. Some letters still leap out of the files and bite me. There are a few angry exchanges. There's a long cry of pain from a writer we prized but who had heard gossip that made her think otherwise – and who sacked us on the spot. There's a book with too many typefaces that looks like a dog's breakfast. The first edition of *The Children's Bach* has a typo in the last sentence – proofread by at least three of us, with tears in our eyes, we told the author later in feeble explanation. There's a letter in the files from Rod Jones forgiving us for failing to submit *Julia Paradise* to one of the major awards, when it had a real chance of winning. And we knew Rod needed the money badly.

We were acutely aware that our authors could have had bigger advances and marketing budgets elsewhere than we could give them – and that may have made us try harder. We were slugging it out with the big boys in public. Behind the scenes we were making it up as we went along, training people without much experience, developing a way of working editorially that included empathy along with process.

Carmel Bird was commissioned to write a manual for aspiring writers, which she did in a series of letters of great clarity which she called *Dear Writer*.

> You must trust your ear and your heart. This is no easy matter, but takes time and courage, vigilance

and confidence . . . Your sentence must lead the reader up to the meaning so that the meaning can dawn like light in the reader's mind.[12]

We worked with writers in the office whenever we possibly could, and by letter and telephone when no one could afford to travel. Usually we managed to arrange at least an initial conversation face-to-face. We learnt to ask questions, make suggestions – and to do the first edit in pencil. This was a useful reminder, for ourselves, that the editorial process was secondary to the act of writing, and, for authors, that the text remained in their charge and that they must in the end seek solutions for themselves. Suggestions could be ignored, and often they were. But by our indicating the places in the work where the writing seemed uneven, the voice wavered or the reader's attention wandered – often a sign of something going wrong – the author would find a way to solve the problem.

Mostly I look at the books from that time and remember the pleasure – but we had our share of difficult authors like everybody else. One writer brought us her first novel in a folder with each page safely sleeved in plastic, told us it was perfect, and produced examples of the typeface and cover image she required. All it needed was a fast track to the printer. But she learned to trust us after a while. There was the occasional person whose ego raged out of control – *Don't touch a comma* – but their opposite number, *You fix it for me*, also needed careful handling.

One or two men described themselves as geniuses and made it clear they thought we were lucky to have them. Editorial suggestions, especially from women, were occasionally interpreted as wilful weakening of the masterpiece. Publishers had never given them the support they desired or the sales figures they deserved. Reviews were always by people who had an axe to grind. In a tussle over hardback and paperback formats one genius declared that he didn't care if only twelve people read his novel, as long as they were the right twelve.

Other problems sometimes arose on publication. One writer couldn't bear to open his parcel of advance copies for several weeks and then disappeared when the first radio interview threatened. Another refused all interviews on publication but then complained about her sales. Another started speaking of *my publicist* as if she were a personal slave, then felt free to give her a hard time. One bloke, we later discovered, had sold his cover artwork to a mate in the pub. There were a few who couldn't deal with the sight of their editor or publicist working with someone other than themselves – a problem in an office like ours where conversations were fairly public. Gradually we learnt to deflect the damage and minimize over-dependency – mainly, I think, by talking about it amongst ourselves. It didn't happen often. But some contracts had been signed before we realized what we'd let ourselves in for – or the work was too good to refuse.

Although we published and employed men from

the start, we were sometimes caricatured as feminist publishers by the media and more often by our competitors, which might have made them feel better. And we did have to deal occasionally with unreal expectations raised by our being a publishing house run by women, expected to support the movement, reminded of our responsibility to provide a conduit for our sisters in publishing collectives. Once or twice the writers we published copped feminist-inspired criticism – their women characters liked the smell of fresh washing or let men off the hook – and the occasional angry letter took us to task as defenders of male chauvinism for publishing them. But I don't remember ever working with a woman writer who categorized herself as genius – perhaps because the word had been gendered long ago. Uncertainty, a need for reassurance, was rather more likely.

Helen Garner's *The Children's Bach*, published in 1984, is considered by many to be her finest work of fiction to date. Don Anderson, academic and critic, in the *National Times* wrote: 'There are four perfect short novels in the English language. They are, in chronological order, Ford Madox Ford's *The Good Soldier*, Scott Fitzgerald's *The Great Gatsby*, Hemingway's *The Sun Also Rises* and Helen Garner's *The Children's Bach*.'[13]

During the writing of *The Children's Bach* Helen

had left me one of her notes. 'Called in to say that I've put the novel aside for the moment and am pouring out a weird tale called *Postcards from Surfers* which makes me burst into tears nearly every day . . . it sure is *dragging* the fucking *pond*.'

By now Helen's stories and her journalism were being widely sought after and regularly published. Publishers elsewhere were asking for reading copies. Ginger Barber placed *The Children's Bach* in the States and eventually Bloomsbury in London, which found the novel too short for one of their handsome hardback fiction volumes, bought the rights to Helen's stories, *Postcards from Surfers* – which had been published in 1985. Bloomsbury then produced a combined edition.

With the Bloomsbury publication of *Postcards from Surfers* and *The Children's Bach*, Helen's position as one of the best stylists of her generation was finally secure in the UK. The *Guardian* called it 'an exceptional, triumphant collection . . . which climbs with easy fluent precision to an eagle's eye view of life . . .'[14] The *New York Times Book Review* in 1986 spoke of '. . . her idiosyncratic vision, her controlled lyricism, and a goodly variety of feisty characters who insist on having their say . . . her sharp strange images and the dense rich texture their layering makes.'

That same year Helen gave an interview to the *Australian Women's Weekly* and spoke about novel writing being 'like trying to make a patchwork quilt look seamless. A novel is made up of scraps of our own lives and bits of other people's, and things we

think of in the middle of the night and whole notebooks full of randomly collected details . . .'[15]

Helen's notebooks were well known, as was her
habit of turning aside from a conversation and jotting
down parts of an exchange. *Monkey Grip* had been
published to rumblings amongst some of the inhabitants of her Carlton milieu that they were thinly
disguised and their stories 'appropriated'. But later,
when Ken Cameron auditioned for the film of
Monkey Grip, several people hot-footed it to Sydney
insisting on the right to play themselves.

Helen's stories are always dissected for details from
her own and other people's lives. *The Children's Bach*
was no exception. She freely admitted that some of
the characters were closely based on friends of hers,
to whom she showed the manuscript before publication. One or two people, who knew the family, were
outraged on their behalf and attempted to talk us out
of publishing the book, not, I think, because of what
was *said*, but because they were offended by the blur-
ring of the boundaries between the real and the
imagined. The couple depicted behaved with dignity
and their friendship with Helen survived. She treats
her own life with much the same openness and lack
of caution. Her writings, fiction and journalism,
impart a sense of her thinking aloud, the blood
beneath the skin – and her readership responds to the
integrity and truth of it.

and Dexter will sit on the edge of the bed to do up
his sandals, and Athena will creep over to him and

put her head on his knee, and he will take her head
in his hands and stroke it with a firm touch,

and the tea will go purling into the cup.[16]

Tim, Denise and Jesse Winton spent much of 1987
and 1988 in France, Ireland and Greece and the files
are full of telexes and long letters and postcards as
Tim dealt with proofs and illustrators trying out
cover ideas for *Minimum of Two*, *In the Winter Dark*
and *Jesse*. When *In the Winter Dark* was published in
1988 after a long period of working and reworking
there were signs that some reviewers were becoming agitated by Tim's plainspeaking Christianity. It
got up the noses of some critics who found his
Protestant imagery irritating and at odds with their
own religious symbolism. Winton's iconography
was 'like a Georges' Christmas window', one critic
sneered – Georges then being a department store
given to displays of elegant baubles. He was accused
of 'hick Satanism' by another; another wrote that
'We [cannot] see the grace of any God worth both-
ering with.' But responses to religious imagery, like
literary judgements, are highly subjective and other
reviewers thought the book his finest so far. The
bad reviews must have hurt horribly, and we hated
sending them to Greece, but by then Tim on Hydra
had begun work on *Cloudstreet*.

Tim's great gift is his ability to reach readers of all ages and degrees of sophistication. It's the *point*, as it were, of his having the gift of the story-telling gab, a kind of mission in his life. He had an unusually clear sense of his readership right from the start, it seemed to me, and it was not 'only' a literary one. Tim's goal is quite clear – to touch the widest number of readers through story. He has the capacity, rare in any writer, to cross markets and generations, and not sweat about damaging his literary credentials.

His American publishers after his first US book tour reported how astonished they'd been at what Tim was prepared to give of himself – in bookshops, on campuses, at endless readings and signings around the country. It seems to me he has always understood that his work strikes deep chords in his readers and he is meticulous about honouring them.

In London in September 1987, before Frankfurt, I'd been invited to lunch with Graham C. Greene, Chairman of Chatto, Cape and Bodley Head and of the International Publishers Association in London. He took me to the Gay Hussar in Greek Street and quizzed me gently on our plans and perspectives for southern hemisphere publishing. I was suitably charmed and warmed, and, of course, rang Diana to speculate on the conversation.

What was going on here? Was it just a courtesy to

a visiting publisher from Australia? Was it the kind of flattery we were used to? You two are doing such *marvellous* publishing. *Wonderful* authors. *Clever* Penguin to have you . . . Or was it just possible that the opportunities for growth in Australia, that many people believed were there for the asking for the CCBH Group, were now being focused on under the new ownership? That my wait in the rain hadn't been in vain after all? And that an established publishing base in Australia was the best place to start? This was a Group that had published great books for many years. Its authors included Toni Morrison, Ian McEwan, Bruce Chatwin, A.S. Byatt, Michael Holroyd, Doris Lessing, our own David Malouf and Patrick White.

While I was still in London, Rupert Murdoch bought a fifteen per cent share of the Pearson Group which included Penguin. There was some alarm about this, Diana wrote, but not as much as the rumours that were flying around at Penguin about the 'known but not yet official departure of Brian . . . The general feeling is of enormous outside forces gathering behind our little leap into the future.'

Then one afternoon in October, about a month later, Graham C. Greene, King of British publishing, personification of the English literary tradition, nephew of Graham Greene even, arrived at our offices. After an exchange of kisses and mutual admiration, he described for us some of the Group's plans for Australia to develop a more active publishing presence. Then he leant back on one of our ancient office couches and said delicately, 'Why don't you join us?' A proposal whereby Random House might acquire shares in McPhee Gribble and McPhee Gribble become Random House's publishing arm in Australia was outlined as one of several possibilities. Of course, 'McPhee Gribble would continue to develop its own fine list of authors' but publish alongside them selected UK and US authors in the Group.

What Graham C. Greene was now talking about seemed to be just what we were working towards – a fully fledged publishing presence that could select and publish, not merely promote and distribute, the books in the combined lists of a group such as Chatto, Cape and Bodley Head, where Australian books and British, American and European titles were properly published. A *bridge between cultures*, was how Harvill's Christopher MacLehose once described the best kind of publishing house.

A week later, at his request, we wrote to Graham C. Greene, by now back in London, 'Your timing was extraordinary. We are poised to take on a third shareholder and enlarge the list substantially.' Then followed the first of what would become, over the next two awful years, the familiar cloak-and-dagger negotiations via confidential faxes timed to arrive at the office before start of business, or late-night phone calls.

We were asked to clarify our arrangements with Penguin Books Australia and Diana summed them up neatly. 'Terms savage but reasonable giving us access to the best distribution in Australia and now showing signs of restricting its services to the Penguin Group. They have gone to great lengths to assure us they see us as part of the "family" and would be pained and surprised to know that we see ourselves as moderately well-fed houseguests with a door key and a fast car in the driveway.'

Then a slightly ominous *Strictly Private and Confidential* letter arrived from Greene. 'We will come back to you swiftly . . . so you are not left in limbo too long . . . We all admire what you have achieved and it would be a privilege to work with you.'[17] After sitting up all night crunching numbers and speculating on marketing plans, we were well past the point where compliments were gratifying. A week later came a phone call from Chief Executive Simon Master saying they would *of course* want to buy our stock out from Penguin. Then a week later, the inevitable flannelling began: 'I owe you a word . . .' and 'Hope to be in touch early next week' until, not at all to our surprise, on 7 December, from Graham C. Greene: 'I fear it's no go. Too many things going on at once. Very disappointed.'

So were we. The prospect of colleagues in London such as Carmen at Chatto, Sonny Mehta at Knopf, Tom Maschler and others at Cape and the Bodley Head who were book people to the core, several of whom we knew were also wanting to build something formidable in Australia, had been a seductive glimpse of what a fully fledged Australian publishing operation might be.

Our sense of urgency and foreboding grew as the

stock market collapsed in the middle of October 1987. The worst effects were to come some months later when the government would put the brakes on in an attempt to slow inflation, but all the indications were there that the economy had been shaken to its foundations and investment capital would soon start to dry up. In December, Brian Johns resigned from Penguin, as was anticipated, to head the Special Broadcasting Service, and the writing was on the wall. Earlier that year Trevor Glover had left Australia to run Penguin UK and several people at Penguin warned us that our co-publishing deal was likely to be renegotiated if Johns was to leave. We were well aware of mounting tensions. The co-publishing deal, a security blanket in so many ways, was a publisher-to-publisher arrangement. Without the shared belief in the books we were doing and the mutual goodwill we'd enjoyed with Brian for four years, we would soon be in dire straits.

7

A Break in the Narrative

Just before Easter in 1988, Elaine Markson rang me. Elaine was one of the New York agents we worked with as we sought more American titles for the list, but she also represented Rodney Hall, whose international reputation was growing. Rodney, Elaine said, wanted to move from Penguin to McPhee Gribble with his next novel. Rodney Hall had been published by Penguin in Australia since *Just Relations* in 1982 but had not been happy with the way his last book, *Kisses of the Enemy*, had been positioned. This was a difficult novel, perhaps not his best – but Faber and Farrar, Straus were his publishers in London and New York and we would be delighted to have him. There was always the chance that any author might simply be wanting to change publishers in the hope of a more compliant editorial arrangement, but we knew Rodney and felt sure we could work together.

The manuscript of *Captivity Captive* arrived and I read it at Easter beside the Big River in Northern Victoria where Don and I were camping. While he fished for trout I read what was, to me, the best novel Rodney had yet written, a story of a ghastly murder in the forests of the south coast of NSW in 1898.

> The paddock where they lay violated and shot, two of them together and Norah separate at the foot of a spotted-gum, stood quiet with that buzzing muffled hush of something you will never forget . . . thick from the horror that had been there, frogs dumb for a whole day after the shock of a lifetime.[1]

Back in the office, I rang Bruce Sims at Penguin and let him know we'd been told that Rodney Hall was on the move and that we wanted to make an offer for him. Bruce, Rodney's editor, was realistic, as he always is, and constructive. Penguin would still profit from the turnover from the novel, as he pointed out. McPhee Gribble would look after Rodney. No great harm would be done. Surely.

Diana and I did our sums, sweated on the size of the advance required, made Elaine Markson an offer which was accepted. *Captivity Captive* would be sold around the world on three separate contracts. Rodney would be offered editorial comments by three editors, Robert McCrum from Faber, Pat Strachan from Farrar, Straus and me, and would choose to follow our suggestions as he saw fit. The publishers could share some of the costs of a hardback printing.

Rodney was in China and sent us a telegram saying how pleased he was. So were we. It was all highly satisfactory. This was how international literary publishing could and should work in a relationship of equals, each enthused by an author's work and benefiting from the others' involvement. A casebook example of rights splitting.

A few days later Penguin sought an urgent meeting to discuss our co-publishing arrangement. Managing Director Peter Field, Susan Ryan, a former Minister in the Hawke government, who had recently replaced Brian Johns as Publishing Director, and Bruce Sims met in our office. Somewhat to our surprise, the meeting had been called to remind us of our status as very junior partners in an arrangement that the company 'now was reconsidering'. It was clear that the anger generated by the transfer of an author – even one Penguin regarded as rather hard to please and not a huge money-maker – had, if not caused the shift in attitude, at least triggered it.

A few months earlier we had published Morris Lurie's fine autobiography, *Whole Life*. Morris was an author who changed publishers regularly. He had been with Penguin on and off before he moved to McPhee Gribble – and would return to Penguin soon afterwards. This may have contributed to the implication underlying the meeting that a haemorrhage of Penguin's authors could happen any day. This was absurd. We knew it. Bruce knew it. His authors were intensely loyal to him. Susan Ryan, new to the game, may have been concerned, but I doubt it. The majority of Penguin authors were securely in place – and, in any case, *if they are dissatisfied, we don't want them* seemed to be Penguin's attitude to those who were critical of their handling. For some mysterious reason, a shabby little pink publishing house, paying its way but only just, had crossed some mark in the sand. We had got too big for our boots. We were warned that Penguin 'could not tolerate their authors going to us' since we 'had nothing different to offer'.[2] A reconsideration of the co-publishing arrangement, we were told, could 'blow us out of the water' – as well we knew. We'd been trying to secure our future for the past year.

We had already begun expanding the list in order to publish in more formats other than Penguin's and to be in a position to attract investors. A Sydney office had been established in a minute cottage in McGarvie Street, Paddington as an inexpensive solution to interstate travel and promotion costs. This was a place where staff or writers on promotion tours could stay overnight. Friend and author Robert Drewe was offered a writing room and a commission from us to spot new talent.

Comedy and political satire were hugely popular during the long years of the Hawke Labor government and several books were commissioned from leading comic writers and performers – at least partly because they made us laugh. Ignatius Jones came up with a guide to *True Hip*. Red Symons was slaving over his *Little Red Book of Naughty* for children and John Rothfield was bringing us in chapters of his *Dr Turf's Guide to Better Punting*. 'There's only one way to enjoy punting and it's called winning.'

Kaz Cooke was writing her *Modern Girl's Guide to Everything* and *The Modern Girl's Guide to Safe Sex*. 'As if life for a Modern Girl wasn't busy enough already, with trying to run our lives, looking out for Mr Right while we gallivant around with Mr Approximates, saving up for the perfect pair of red shoes and remembering not to get pregnant. Now we have to know about diseases as well.'[3]

Peter Cundall's *The Practical Australian Gardener* was in production and Jim Morgan's fine first novel *Parakeet*, about old pastoral families in the South Australian outback, was being edited at this time. Helen Daniel was delivering sections of her comprehensive *Good Reading Guide*, a survey of Australian writing based on the rather unusually sympathetic principle of constructive rather than destructive criticism. And Stephanie Alexander was discussing with us her plans to do a massive guide, arranged by ingredients to all the bounty of regional Australian food.[4]

Our production department had grown and, now that we were publishing as often as we could in formats other than Penguin paperbacks, the look of the books became much more individual and original. Mary Callahan, a young designer straight out of college, joined us, and my eldest son, a trainee graphic designer, was learning how to prepare finished art. Our first real colophon – a beautiful, slightly ambiguous Celtic knot – at last began to replace the penguin on all our books.

In June Penguin Books Australia gave us formal notice of a change in terms. The time frame was

generous, the letters courteous, commonsense prevailed. We were given plenty of time to go out and
refinance ourselves, and start all over again – in a
severe economic downturn that was worsening by
the week.

Then began one of the most difficult periods which
any small company with limited resources can face.
The publishing profile of the company, the growth of
the programme and the fledgling international list had
to be kept high – as did morale. We were working as
closely as ever with our authors. Somehow we had to
keep our escalating problems confidential.

Publishing thrives on gossip. We were in the public eye now more than ever. The media profiles from
that time are full of our optimism and plans for the
future. Even the *TLS* described our 'authentic
vision'.[5] Authors and agents were rating us for design,
editorial and contractual arrangements above larger
companies, but our turnover was fragile because so
many of our retail prices and our backlist titles were
still locked to Penguin's. I often found myself thinking of John Michie's dark maxim, that *if the literary
community starts praising you, you must be doing something wrong.*

The archives become clogged at this point with five-
year business plans and spreadsheets. They make
depressing reading. Even now they exude for me

tension and a dreadful kind of side-tracking. There was no way out. Company profiles, marketing plans, explanations of what we were trying to achieve and why we needed to refinance ourselves at this bad time – all were necessary and well done, but not enough.

We spent much time inventing imaginary publishing programmes. The sums went something like this: Take the reality of authors under contract and multiply them three times for expansion and 'improved productivity', add a dose of caution to allow for late deliveries and titles that might never be written since authors sometimes change their minds, factor in the mounting returns rate from bookshops as interest rates bite, add the fact the authors' advances everywhere were doubling every year. Turn around three times under a full moon and pray.

I think Diana and I both knew how fragile the projections were, but they were essential as we embarked on round after round of meetings with potential investors, equity partners, financial advisers and assorted cowboys. We wore our best clothes. We listened to lots of advice. Some of it was helpful, much of it was based on misreadings of the publishing industry which has its own idiosyncrasies, imponderables and awkward timeframes. These were hard to explain to the money men. And, perhaps, particularly to Australian money men sitting across the desk from two women. We were called 'girls' often and sometimes it seemed to me that the connections of fathers and uncles carried more weight than the idea of investing in the steady growth of a publishing house with a reasonable track record. There were no precedents we could draw on and we found ourselves describing Bloomsbury's successful financing in London, for want of an Australian example, to unimpressed Australian merchant bankers wanting considerable start-up fees and 17.5 per cent interest rates.

The questions they put to us over and over again were revealing. Why should an author take two years to write a book? Can't you put a rocket under them? Why pay advances on royalties which might be out-standing for years? Why carry stock of titles? Why not print on demand? Why keep books in print if the author has another on the way? Why not cut the staff in half and stop what we regarded as essential invest-ment in work-in-progress? Why not do different kinds of books altogether? A sports series was sug-gested, as was publishing a list of pornography which one young investment broker had heard was a prof-itable line. Somehow we soldiered on.

The books we were publishing, the authors who were sending us their work as it unfolded – always the books kept me going. I don't know what kept Diana going. She never told me. The unimaginable had happened. I think we had gone into panic at the same time and were unable to help each other.

It was like being split down the middle, unable to confide in the authors or any of the people we worked with. I am struck now, reading the files and living it all again, by the immense effort we were both making at this time to look like nothing was wrong while we ran the gauntlet of meetings with men in pinstriped suits.

The files are full of coincidences and ironies. Dates on letters full of affection and enthusiasm coincide with meetings that had the power to save us. Occasionally a letter arrived from someone who had picked up a note of the tension we were under – but later friends said they had no idea. Dorothy Hewett had begun sending us her autobiography, *Wildcard*, which Virago and McPhee Gribble had contracted to co-publish.

> The first house sits in the hollow of the heart, it will never go away. It is the house of childhood become myth, inhabited by characters larger than life whose murmured conversations whisper and tug at the mind.[6]

Whole chapters of *Wildcard* would come through the fax overnight and we'd find them in tight rolls of shiny fax paper all over the floor, sometimes mixed up with proposals and counter-proposals from brokers and bankers.

Already by early 1988 Drusilla Modjeska was letting me read chapters in draft of her portrait of her mother. This was another of the rich friendships and conversations of my publishing life – not at all an editorial process, it was far too early for that, but the privilege of watching a highly imaginative work gradually emerge and find its voice.

> The first wound comes with the cutting of the umbil-
> ical cord. The thread is cut and we're out there alone.
> Where? I don't know, I didn't recognize a thing,
> bright and light with rain pebbling the windows.
>
> In my family there have been three generations of
> daughters first born, and in each case the mother
> wept and outside the rain settled in, as if in sympathy.
> Well, it was England, it's not so surprising.[7]

I had not seen elsewhere what was happening in some Australian non-fiction writing. The divide between fact and fiction was being addressed. There was a readiness to set aside the rules, the safety-nets of conventional methodology, and treat the reader as an intimate. The uncertainties of the biographer, the silences and gaps in the record, were being given their due rather than papered over. *Poppy* would be one of those books that would mark a major change in Australian writing.

Helen Garner was by now living in Sydney after the filming of her screenplay *The Last Days of Chez Nous*. She was writing her next novel, *Cosmo Cosmolino*, in Drusilla Modjeska's house in Newtown and I missed them both. Helen sent me another note. 'My sentences have got longer. It's much more fun to wrestle long ones to the mat, even if bits of them are still sticking up behind my shoulder.'

She was happier than I'd seen her for a long time,

in a relationship with novelist Murray Bail, whose work couldn't have been more different from her own. I worried briefly, as did many of Helen's friends, about her writing being forced into new shapes. But the pages she sent were spare and shapely. She was still drawing on life and taking the sort of risks with herself that had characterized her writing from the start.

Tim Winton wrote to us from Hydra, as the family left Greece to return home in October 1988: 'We've had a great time here, gotten ourselves tanned, relaxed, with-child, with-book.' Harry was born in May 1989 and *Cloudstreet* would start to arrive in draft soon after.

> Oh, the water has never been so quiet. Quick and Fish and their father move through it like it's a cloud, an idea, just a rumour of water, and when Fish goes down there isn't a sound. Quick feels the net go slack. Lester Lamb smells woodsmoke from the beach; he hears his heart paddling slowly along, but nothing else.[8]

One weekend Murray Bail arrived, persuaded by Helen to show us his writer's notebook which he'd kept years before as a record of his early travels and his reflections on his beginnings as a fiction writer. There were no precedents for publishing such things in Australia, and this, together with Bail's well-known horror of revealing himself in the first person, meant that we had to work hard to convince him that an adjunct to the rest of his fiction should be published at all. I had a slight suspicion that Robert McCrum's enthusiasm for the notebook at Faber carried more weight than ours – Faber was at last considering sharing an edition – but whatever it was we signed up *Longhand*. Persuading Murray to use the first person plural occasionally took a little longer. Faber passed, but eventually we heard from Helen that, 'MB is very happy with the look of his new book. It has a kind of ageless, dateless quality we all agree, the design that is!'

Then, after many years of silence which I'd put down to his sorry experience of being edited by me in 1973, Gerald Murnane wrote one day saying that he had decided he would like to be published, when he was ready, by McPhee Gribble. Murnane had several novels published in the meantime, *The Plains* and *Inland* being perhaps the best; and *Scripsi*, one of the most influential literary magazines of the eighties, had regularly published his stories. I wrote back to Gerald: 'We've been wanting to be your publishers from the start so you'll understand how pleased we are that you've given us your next book.'

The letter strikes me now, in some ways, as characteristic of the office. I was probably the only one who had been waiting and hoping that Murnane would eventually find a reason to come to McPhee Gribble. But 'we' and 'our' had always been a kind of shorthand, first for Diana and me, and then, because it expressed us as a group, it became part of the way we trained people and presented ourselves to the

world. The first person singular was avoided whenever possible, but for rather different reasons from
Murray Bail's. 'Our thoughts', 'our decisions', 'we
will', 'we won't', 'we love your book'. The language
of the place expressed a way of working which had
grown up over the years.

Some time in the middle of all the meetings, when
our distress was high, Harold Bridger arrived. 'He
alighted on the office like an elderly angel,' Meredith
said later. Bridger, a psychoanalyst with a special
interest in family companies and creative work
around the world, was on one of his regular visits to
Australia and had read about us.

The press continued to write about the company
as if it were going from strength to strength, and
Diana and I spoke of it publicly always in the same
vein. Some of the articles make painful reading.
When critic Peter Craven wrote an article describing
McPhee Gribble as 'a partnership made in Heaven',
it felt like a bad joke – but the warmth of his
acknowledgement of what we were doing meant a
great deal. Then we were interviewed for a book
called *Women of Power* – which was not even funny.
I'd never felt more powerless.

Harold Bridger had founded the Tavistock Institute
in London after the war with psychoanalyst Donald
Winnicott, where they developed ways of working

therapeutically with victims of shell shock. He was another of those rare Englishmen who happened to be interested in Australia – the context we were operating in, and Australia's place in the world. He spent several months each year in Melbourne working with companies, and the rest travelling between corporations and groups in the States and Europe. His view of workplaces, whether huge family companies with their sometimes conflicting visions, or volunteer groups supporting drug addicted teenagers, had more to do with metaphors than organization charts. Publishing interested him as a means of transmission, one of the ways ideas and imagination move through the world – not merely as a series of processes which make and sell product.

Harold came to see us whenever he was in Melbourne, and, talking to him, it became very clear how great was our state of dislocation. The pressures we were reeling under were all too obvious. As an independent company in a country crippled by high interest rates at the bottom of the world, McPhee Gribble was in grave danger of failing. The conditions we were trying to contend with could well be impossible to overcome. I think that I faced this now for the first time.

The books felt far more real to me than anything else. When Geoffrey Bardon arrived at the office with

Judith Ryan, Curator of Aboriginal Art at the National Gallery of Victoria, they were carrying boxes of transparencies of magnificent paintings, the early work of the great Aboriginal painters from Papunya in the Western Desert. Some of the pictures were still in Bardon's possession, many were now in major art collections around the country.

Here was *Man's Water Dreaming* by Old Walter Tjampitjinpa, completed in 1971, and the *Children's Water Dreaming* with Possum Story, completed in 1973 by Old Mick Tjakamarra, one of the earliest examples of the dotting method used to express topography. There was Clifford Possum Tjapaltjarri's *Honey Ant Dreaming*, completed in 1972, several paintings by Tim Leura Tjapaltjarri, including his *Sun, Moon and Morning Star* of 1973 – and there was Kaapa Tjampitjinpa's *Wild Orange Dreaming*, painted in 1971.

Geoffrey Bardon's story, diffidently told, of his time at Papunya was entrusted to us in a draft manuscript he had been working on for many years. As a young schoolteacher in 1971 Bardon was posted to what was then an Aboriginal Reserve under white control at Papunya where more than one thousand people lived in a state of extreme dislocation and degradation, held in contempt by many of the whites working there. Although the traditional sand mosaic markings of the Western Desert were well known to anthropologists, there had been no real attempt to ensure their cultural survival or to interpret their meanings.

Bardon's empathy and his affectionate encouragement of the children's drawing slowly won the confidence of the elders and he thought to give the men paints to work with. One man, Kaapa Tjampitjinpa, had been painting on scrap wood and fibro sheets before Bardon arrived at Papunya but had been dismissed as schoolyard man for stealing brushes. 'The painting movement was built around this man's compulsive will and extraordinary ability to paint,' Bardon wrote later. One night a group of Aboriginal men filed into his room.

'I first saw Kaapa Tjampitjinpa, himself. He secretively handed a piece of paper to Old Mick Tjakamarra and kept whispering and making signs to Mick to hand the paper to me.' Bardon heard the word 'design' and realized that the drawing on the piece of paper 'was the first conceptualisation of the great honey ant mural, the first public affirmation of Aboriginal culture at Papunya'. A few days later they gathered beside the school wall.

> It was quite a moment, as we all watched – Old Bert, Old Mick, Bill Stockman and Long Jack and the others – the first hieroglyph being put on the wall lovingly and beautifully, with a marvellous painting technique. Some of the men went across and touched the wall even before the paint had dried. Then little children came across and stood beside the old painting men and Kaapa, and we all stood back and watched the start of the honey ant mural as it was finally to appear. This was the beginning of the Western Desert painting movement, when, led by Kaapa, the Aboriginal men saw themselves in their

own image before their very eyes, on a European
building. Something strange and marvellous was set
in motion.[9]

The art world recognized what had leapt into life
in those years – one of the most remarkable beginnings in modern times of a painting movement – but
Geoffrey Bardon's story was little understood. He had
paid a great price. His role in encouraging the men
to paint and supplying them with canvas and other
materials had unnerved officialdom. He was forced
after a few years to leave Papunya and battled illness
for a long time. But the manuscript he had written
was the result of many years' custodianship and reflec-
tion. Its intuitive and highly informed readings of the
technique and symbology of the pictures brought
together a number of strands of tentative understand-
ings – and *Papunya Tula, Art of the Western Desert*
would be published in 1991.

When eventually Geoffrey Bardon sat down with
the artists in their country nearly twenty years after
his first time there, he gave the old men advance
copies of the book and watched as they were passed
from hand to hand. 'They pored over the images
utterly absorbed and exhilarated,' Bardon said later, 'as
if a great circle of frustration had been completed and
would now be overcome.'

McPhee Gribble was still trying to find an Australian investor, revising the business plan, crunching the numbers. The spreadsheets with their ever-changing sets of projections and imaginary publishing programmes festooned the front offices. We were looking for a real solution not a bail-out, but perhaps we should have raised the alarm long before we did. There were dozens of *shoulds* – and for a long time afterwards I had to force myself not to list them.

There were several glimmers of interest from non-publishing sources. But each time we attempted to convey our value and explain our predicament, we came up against reluctance to invest in what were now being called the *cultural industries*, coralled in a problem category of their own.

The publishing and export market we were establishing was not an aberration or a luxury. Certainly we required an investor with a commitment to quality and steady growth rather than quick returns, prepared to make long-term investment in research and development. None of these featured prominently in the economic rhetoric of the late eighties. To make matters worse, the recession had now hit Australia with a vengeance. The weekly sales reports from Penguin were showing that bookshops were suffering, orders were dropping and the reprint programmes which had long sustained us slowed to a trickle. We increased our overdraft with the bank, secured by us both as best we could.

By mid-year 1989 we both agreed that we had no option but to offer ourselves for sale. This meant, for the first time, putting a monetary value on the company. More meetings. The tangible assets were measurable – the stock, the contracts, the work-in-progress. The intangible was the goodwill – the reputation of the company, its *popularity in the marketplace* was how the accountants defined it, the *benefit by association gained by a purchaser*.

The door had been left slightly ajar by Random House, which had in the meantime become Random Century, now headed by Anthony Cheetham. Carmen Callil was as enthusiastic as ever about a working relationship. Simon Master, whenever we'd met since, had made faintly encouraging noises. One night we rang him. More figures, more fine-tuning of the business plan and forecasts, more enthusiastic voices ringing from the other side of the world, more *For Your Eyes Only* faxes first thing in the morning and late-night phone calls from us carefully explaining our position and our plans.

'The Board members are *terribly* keen on the idea of joining forces with McPhee Gribble,' said Anthony Cheetham. 'It makes absolute sense,' said John Mottram, a director of Century Hutchinson. The original idea was revived that we would publish, in addition to our Australian programme, select titles from the London lists. Carmen was helpful and encouraging, but she warned us what we were up against.

We knew we were arguing from the weakest possible bargaining point but even then when the offer came through we were shocked. We would retain twenty per cent equity in McPhee Gribble and, in exchange for refinancing the company, Random Century would pay us $1.00 for eighty per cent of the shares, for the goodwill of the company, and provide us with the working capital we needed. When we attempted to argue with Cheetham and Master we were quickly put in our place. Any discussion of terms was evidently not on. Our goodwill was worthless.

Our financial adviser at this time, a young South African, was also appalled and offered to telephone Master and go through the figures again, bloke to bloke. He reported back the next morning that there was *a big problem*. We were *lovely ladies* apparently, but *strong individualists* and there were *serious reservations about fit*. And by 20 September the offer was withdrawn on the grounds that we were *too far apart*. Carmen's version was more acerbic. We had not known that she had been locked at the same time in mortal combat with Anthony Cheetham to prevent the extinction of Chatto. 'They can't handle me,' she said, 'and they didn't want three of us.'

By October we had nowhere else to go. We probably never had. Penguin was waiting in the wings, no doubt fully aware of what we were up to, having asked for our three-year forecast a few weeks earlier. Overnight we were made two offers – one for the assets of the company only, not enough by this time to cover our borrowings, and a slightly larger offer for the assets plus me under contract for two years to ensure that the authors came too.

There was no choice. It was a done deal. And of course the authors would come. Penguin was a desirable home for the list. This was just another transfer of copyrights from a small independent imprint to a large successful company. It was happening everywhere, was how we tried to explain it to the staff that day. This was the hardest part. After everyone had gone home we sat in the empty office and cried.

The Sale of Assets of McPhee Gribble Publishers was concluded on the morning of 30 November 1989. The assets were several hundred titles currently under contract, the name of the company, the stock-in-trade, the work-in-progress and whatever remnants remained of the goodwill.

Any victor worth his salt exerts his authority immediately. We were asked to draft an enthusiastic announcement for Penguin to release to the press that evening, then we spent the afternoon ringing the authors.

An eerie silence fell over the office during the next few days. The phones didn't ring. In Melbourne people sent flowers as if we were dead. Then agent Rose Creswell rang and said that Sydney wanted to give us a party and a week or so later that's what they did.

And of course the story didn't end there. Why would it? The manuscripts arrived more or less on time, the authors sought us out as if nothing had happened. The people at Penguin, some of them old friends, were kind and welcoming. This wasn't the first time for them. One day someone showed me a filing cabinet in a corridor and told me that was all that remained of Greenhouse, Sally Milner's company acquired by Penguin the year before. Greenhouse's books had already been absorbed into another imprint. In March 1990, opening a panel session at Writers' Week on corporate takeovers, Peter Field, Penguin's Managing Director, mused that 'The publishing industry is like a rainforest with a few tall trees creating fertile undergrowth below.'

It took another four years for McPhee Gribble to become a filing cabinet. First we had to dismantle the office and all the paraphernalia of fifteen years talking and publishing. We each took some of the big white coffee cups. The armchairs went with the editors, the sofa that looked retro to Sophie and ugly to me went home with her. The trestles went to teenage children, the dozens of fans and desk lamps were sold and the library was given away. The framed author photos came down off the walls into my shed in cartons where, each time I came across them in later years, they would gaze back at me, growing younger and younger. Finally one weekend, in the empty warehouse, Diana and I laid out the file copies on the floor of everything we had ever published, like a map of something.

Dismantling the physical space was the easy part. I took a long time to stop saying *we* and *our* about every aspect of my working life. For many months afterwards it was hard for me to tell where I began and Diana ended. I would sometimes find myself buying a book with her in mind. I look in the mirror and still occasionally even now catch an echo of her in a hand movement or the way my spectacles slide down my nose.

The paperwork supporting the sale dragged on and on with arguments with Penguin about stock valuations and contract assignments. We lost them all. Diana and Megan Nevett bore the brunt of this while those of us who eventually did 'go with the list' tried to adapt fast. In the brief light-headed period of what felt to me like post-operative shock immediately the sale was finalized, I had managed to convey the not very complicated idea that the books would make more money if their editors and designers could keep working on them. They could come out on schedule as if nothing had happened. Diana had by now parachuted out and made other plans, leaving me the rather battered gold star. So, from an original deal acquiring just me and the contracts, five others moved out of the factory in Cecil Street into a tiny makeshift space in one of Penguin's buildings in South Yarra – just a street away from where we'd first begun.

One of the first tasks the new owners asked of me was to project the income from the list for the next two years – something I'd been doing in my sleep – but now with Penguin's healthy margins rather than our threadbare ones, clearly we'd been well worth buying. Yet, 'There's not a lot here,' I was told when

I first presented *Papunya Tula, Art of the Western Desert*, Murray Bail's *Longhand*, Tim Winton's *Cloudstreet*, Drusilla Modjeska's *Poppy*, Helen Garner's *Cosmo Cosmolino*, Vincent Buckley's *Last Poems*, Gabrielle Lord's *Salt* and Kaz Cooke's *A Modern Girl's Green Diary for 1991* and much else besides. The quality of the work and its likely longevity was now only part of the picture.

Some things didn't change and one or two were better. Grinders, whose coffee we had consumed gallons of from the early Carlton days, offered to make special deliveries. The office and the warehouse at Ringwood were many times the size of the one I remembered, and everyone wore suits. But some couches I'd once been sent to choose covers for were there in one of the offices and the Albert Tucker was still on the wall.

The imprint – the name on the books and the Celtic knot – became more prominent, more clearly McPhee Gribble than it had ever been. It was now a valuable marketing tool and promoted vigorously. The authors didn't visit often, as the space we'd been allotted was too crowded for talk, and I think we didn't want to be seen. But their books were looked after as best we were able. We spent more time in meetings, we filled in a lot more forms, we became adept at costing editorial time, we accepted covers that were seven out of ten. We fell into line and the corporation began to absorb us.

In the midst of the commiserations, the kind letters and faxes and the press coverage bemoaning the loss of *yet another Australian icon*, a few people wrote congratulating us on being bought out – on having achieved a good result. With other colleagues in the publishing industry, we had been arguing all year with Allan Fels, head of the Prices Surveillance Authority, against an open market for books because it would be bad for authors, bad for independent publishers and bad for Australian publishing generally. Independent publishing was fragile enough in Australia without having to cope with the dumping of unsold stock especially from the US that an open market would allow. The spectre we conjured up of rapid collapse and acquisition of independent publishers was exactly what would happen to us within the year.

A month after we'd gone to the wall, Allan Fels sent me a Christmas card wishing me well *in your new home*, and I read it as mocking me. Now I can see that, most likely, Fels would have genuinely thought the natural order had prevailed and that we would be pleased.

The McPhee Gribble story, like all good stories, can be read on several levels. Even I can see that. Tilting at windmills and the feminine versus the masculine workplace are only the most obvious. Being difficult women probably didn't help. As a straightforward economic narrative, of how part of the world works, it has lessons perhaps for today. As I tell the story I am aware that it is a rather neat case study which proves the efficiency of the marketplace, the smooth workings of global capitalism, the consolidation of copyrights. Independent companies operating idiosyncratically with limited resources and big ideas can be reminders of other ways to do things.

Why tell the story after all this time? The depth of my reluctance to find a way to revisit those years surprised me. I had moved on, we all had. In any case it is hard to tell the story of a time and a place that, in so many ways, and by many people, for their own reasons, has become somewhat mythologized. In the scheme of things, the weight of what was achieved, it must be said, was not very great. We lasted fifteen years to Angus & Robertson's eighty as an independent company. Family-owned Thomas Lothian published their first book, Bernard O'Dowd's *The Silent Land and other Verses*, in 1906 and are still going strong. The university presses were publishing Australian scholarly works and textbooks in the long years before anyone else was much interested. Melbourne University Press, the oldest, first published Myra Willard's *History of the White Australia Policy* in 1923, paid for by the author in paper covers at a price of 10/6, the author to receive the proceeds from the sale of 350 copies less ten per cent commission.[10]

When I hear authors speak of being published by

'McPhee Gribble' it sounds to me too good to be true. A poet recently told me he'd once called his cats Gribble and McPhee. David Williamson mentioned us in a play – presumably to signify strong women with power over men's words. Tours of cultural sites, I'm told, sometimes take in our old terrace in Carlton and the warehouse in Fitzroy. The name of the company appears on the CVs of designers and editors as if a job there has bestowed on them great gifts.

I want to protest that it wasn't like that. I want to say that through much good fortune we managed to catch a wave of Australian writing and thinking about this place that hadn't been there in quite that way before. That we were inexperienced and made things up as we went along. That the company was always under-capitalized. That we worked long hours almost every day for fifteen years. That our production manager used to describe her budget and the poorly equipped production department as being like working in Poland. And I remember that what had been an independent publishing house run by two women friends with their own money for fifteen years and the best staff they could find, did not end well.

I am too close to the story to write anything resembling history, too far from it now not to be mindful of Borges' warning that 'forgetfulness and memory are likely to be inventive'. But the McPhee Gribble story did have a beginning, a middle and an end. Its authors have flourished, most of them, and some of the books we published are still around. It was so clearly a creature of its time and place, and my part in it had its origins in every corner of my life, that it occurs to me rather belatedly that perhaps I tell the story now in order to make sense of it to myself. Australia was where we happened to be, what we wanted to be part of as it took on its new shape. And, after all, we were of the generation that thought we could do anything, and for a little while, in a small way, we might have.

Afterwords

In a New York bookshop not long ago, one of those rare places on the planet which still keeps some backlists in stock, I found some Australian books. Here was an ancient copy of Helen Garner's *Monkey Grip* in an old American Seaview edition with the weird dustjacket of Javo the junkie floating above a pounding sea. There were three copies of Peter Carey's *Jack Maggs* in paperback, several copies of Peter Robb's *M, a Biography of Caravaggio* in hardcovers and David Malouf's *The Great World* from Random House. Across the street in another bookstore I found copies of Inga Clendinnen's *Reading the Holocaust* and *The Future Eaters* by Tim Flannery.

In Singapore and Hong Kong recently there was nothing from Australia at all except for lots of Lonely Planet guides, and some picture books introducing Sydney for the Olympics. In Bombay and Madras there may be still a few copies of David Malouf's backlist, Gillian Mears' stories and Libby Hathorn's children's books left over from a writers' tour and published by Penguin India assisted by the Australia Council a few years ago.

In a central London chain last year there was a large pile of the Harvill edition of *Eucalyptus* by Murray Bail next to Coetzee's *Disgrace* and several of Robert Drewe's backlist on the Picador stand next to Colm Tóibín and Hanif Kureishi. Two first-time novelists were there, Julia Leigh's *The Hunter* and Tom Gilling's *The Sooterkin* in Faber. David Marr's *Patrick White: a Life*, published nearly ten years ago now, was still on the shelf in a Vintage paperback, and several big glossy picture books of the Dreamtime which I hadn't seen in Australia and which may have been a package put together after a Frankfurt Book Fair, where books about Aboriginal dot paintings are now in much demand.

Not a lot has changed.

What has changed is the way the money works and the fact that working with writers editorially is not considered smart business any more. It doesn't fit current notions of efficient corporate structures. And most writers, upon whose copyrights the whole edifice rests, do not fit them either. Writers everywhere have always done it hard. Some are adjusting to the new environment. A few are thriving and are well rewarded. Others, unless we recognize their intrinsic value and fragility, must seek other ways to get what they need – places where their voices can find strength and where they have the freedom to write nuanced prose out of their differences and out of where they are.

The controls on what is published are now more subtle and more pervasive than the old censorship. Book publishing has become part of the media. Publishing directors state their independence – and indeed, if the Board is satisfied that the shareholders' money invested is working as hard as it should be, they have a certain freedom to shape 'their' lists. But risk must be minimized, return on capital realized rapidly. Commissions that don't take too long, authors who don't require much attention and can write the sort of product that will sell fast – these are the name of the game.

What was once called *the publishing house* is no longer. Many publishing corporations suffer from a kind of giantism and are not much more than marketing and sales machines. The old maxim rules: the reader is a mug and the writer is a commodity – *Sell 50,000 copies before anyone discovers they're not much good*. And individual creativity and relationships are devalued, marketing rules and the workplace could be trading in stocks or cosmetics rather than in those slippery things called words.

Picture the scene.

It is 6 p.m. on a summer evening in a large city. It is Sydney but it could just as well be somewhere else. The bookshop is one of the best in town, beloved of authors and of readers because its owners understand the importance not only of well-stocked shelves but of good talk about books. Their shop is a hub of literary life, for launches, for readings and afternoons spent browsing the shelves.

This evening it is hot inside. The crowd, dressed mainly in black, spills out onto the footpath. There is white wine in plastic glasses and mineral water with bubbles. The occasion is the launch of a first novel by a writer not yet a household name, but a regular reviewer of contemporary dance for one of the dailies. She is pale and pretty and very nervous. Someone has given her a bunch of flowers. Her family has come from another state and friends have turned out for her. Other writers are there too, as well as her agent, her publicist, and her publisher – another young woman whose list makes news. The crowd is large and it bodes well.

The publisher calls for silence. She describes the day this book arrived on her desk fully formed, how edgy it was, how many boundaries it crossed, how film rights are in negotiation and how the US company in the Group is considering taking copies. The Poms, as usual, she says, have passed. *Laughter.* Then an older writer of novels – famous, but not so famous that it doesn't help his sales to be seen to be generously supporting a younger colleague – gives a little speech. He is warm but oblique, so the audience doesn't quite know what he thinks or even how much he's read of the new book.

The author is pink with pleasure and there's a quiver in her voice as she thanks the older writer, her publicist, the cover designer and finally her friend the publisher who has been, she says, 'supportive and always available when I needed reassurance. I knew I was in good hands.' *More laughing and clapping.*

The new novelist signs copies. That night 120 copies are sold for $25.00 plus GST. The bookshop has taken 250. Total orders from around the country are 2550 on sale or return which means that the books can be returned if they don't sell. The shops will reorder if the demand builds – and the publicity department will try hard for two weeks to see that it does.

The publishing house has printed 4000 copies in a large format paperback. They have paid an advance of $20,000 over two books which means that the new fiction writer received $5000 on signing the contract over a year ago. Her agent has taken fifteen per cent but, as the two-book contract would not have happened without her, and the advance would have been much lower, this is fair.

Three months ago, the new novelist made a presentation to the sales force. Of the twenty novels they were to sell in the next half year, eight were from first-time authors, both in Australia and from the UK. The sales force warmed to her, were pleased she would promote the book, and praised the publisher for the rather erotic-looking advance covers in their sales kits.

On publication day the new novelist is due to receive another $5000. The book has taken the new novelist two years to write. If it sells all 4000 copies, less review copies and publicity advances, and reprints another 2000 copies, she will eventually get another $5000 less fifteen per cent for the agent and twenty-five per cent held by the publisher as a reserve against returns from the bookshops. The figures are a worry.

The budget for publicity is $3000, generous for a new novel, but the Marketing Director believes this one *has legs*. There was a photo shoot early on before editing commenced as the book was to be featured in the summer catalogue. Printed invitations to the launch, a small dinner afterwards and an author tour to two cities took care of the rest.

A junior publicist starts work on the review list. She obtains a profile piece about the author's Australia Council-funded residency in a studio for three months last year in Edinburgh where the voice of the novel was authenticated, the street names checked and something very like the near rape in the last chapter happened. This provides an extra angle for the publicist to offer when placing interviews. The author may be prepared to talk about the rape and name names, the publicist promises. Six radio interviews are lined up for the week of publication.

The editorial budget for the book was set nine months earlier when the publisher argued strongly in

the budget meeting for her annual allocation for freelance work, but instead she was told to limit the
amount of new fiction this year. Her freelance budget
has remained the same for the last three years but
marketing has had a twelve per cent increase. The
publisher is powerless to change this. There is a Publishing Director who is in charge of budgets and the
shape of the list. He manages the 'big' books and the
publisher reports to him. She is not on the Board
where these decisions are made. The Board consists
of the Managing Director, the Marketing Director,
the Sales and Distribution Director, the Finance
Director, the Publishing Director, two outside directors from other media industries and the Chairman.
They report to the overseas Board which is, like most
Australian publishing companies, answerable to
British or American shareholders.

The publisher has allocated $1000 to this novel for
freelance editing. The editor is experienced but is
many hundreds of kilometres away in Adelaide. She
is requested by the publisher to do a light edit for
which she'll be paid the equivalent of about $30 an
hour, for thirty hours. The manuscript is more than
300 pages long. There is no money for reading and
re-reading and discussing possible solutions. She and
the author have never met and phone calls must be
okayed by the publisher.

After reading the manuscript once and making
many notes, the editor sends an email to the publisher recommending that the novel needs more time.
The book is already scheduled and, in any case, *a*

heavy edit isn't called for so extra time is refused. The freelance editor asks for the author's phone number and rings her with some suggestions. These they both know would take months to work through.

The author consults the publisher who says she thinks the freelance editor is over-reacting and that the promotion schedule is already firmed up. The agent, also consulted by the author, is concerned but reminds her that the publisher wants the book out in the shops for Christmas. They both reassure the author that the book is *fantastic.* This is the third time in a year that this freelance editor has alerted an author to the need for a rewrite. The publisher makes a mental note not to use this editor again. The freelance editor has by now spent twenty hours so must copy edit what she has as fast as she can.

The rest of the editorial budget is spent on proof corrections and on a blurb written by the publisher who skims the proofs and raves about it at lunch with the sales manager. Afterwards the publisher reworks the cover copy to give it more market appeal. She adds phrases like *an emotional cliff-hanger* and *groundbreaking.* The cover costs $750 for a photo library still, which a designer has manipulated on screen; the publisher then pays another $800 for the cover design – which features a glorious close-up shot of a marbled spine and shoulder blades rising from what looks like foam. The warm, oblique, older author who will launch the book has been asked for a coverline. He describes the novel as *a lyrical meditation on the essence of life.*

Good Weekend had photographed the new author some weeks earlier sitting in a pretty and writerly old cane chair on a verandah in the Blue Mountains, and the magazine runs a profile piece to coincide with publication. The day after the launch that summer evening, the new novelist was interviewed on 'Arts Today'. She spoke well about her book, she was serious-minded and grateful to her publisher.

I too received my advance copy and my personally signed letter from the publisher telling me that this novel would surely change my life. Already twenty-eight novels, half of them first novels by authors under thirty, had appeared on Australian publishers' lists by mid-year, so the competition was out there. I wanted to believe the publisher's claim that this new novel was *a find*. There are such things.

My concern for this young woman turns out not to be misplaced. The freelance editor was right. The book is uneven. The reviews are unkind. The writer's journalist colleagues are unforgiving. Envious, her friends say, but the book's flaws over-shadow its originality. Most readers give up after page 20 when the main character, declared tiresome by his creator on page 4, becomes too much to bear. The novel needed more consideration by the author after receiving editorial advice she could trust.

Widespread talk about the book, friends recommending it to each other, bookclubs eager to discuss it, doesn't happen. After two months the bookshops start returning copies and in a fortnight 1200 come in from all around the country. About 2500 copies needed to be sold for the publishing company to break even.

A favourable review in a small journal and an inflight magazine which runs photos of the author aren't enough to help. The author's agent rings the publicity department to be told *There's nothing we can do. It's a dog.* The agent is shocked but tells the author that *the publishers are still pushing it.* But she knows they aren't – her local bookshop has copies but David Jones doesn't and Borders has two.

The author is angry and humiliated and blames the publicity department. The agent is angry and blames the freelance editor who hasn't fixed the faults. The publisher is angry because the book won't earn out its advance and there is a contract for a second. The Publishing Director and the sales director will give the publisher a hard time when she reports to the monthly publishing meeting. There will be questions asked about her judgement for the third time this year after she leaves the room. This first novel will sell half its print run, and the author's second book will be published in two or three years with much less enthusiasm.

The book needed more time but the deadline loomed larger than the author's unvoiced need to set the book aside for six months and read it with a fresh eye. She was on a conveyor belt and nobody was free to tell her the truth.

In 1950, in a Commonwealth Literary Fund lecture, Miles Franklin argued for something that barely existed.

> Without an indigenous literature people can remain alien in their own soil. An unsung country does not fully exist or enjoy adequate international exchange in the inner life. Further, a country must be portrayed by those who hate it or love it as their dwelling place, familiarly, or remain dumb among its contemporaries. The fuller its libraries, the louder its radios, the more crowded its periodicals with imported stories and songs, the more clearly such dependence exposes innate poverty.[1]

Now I think we must visit all over again what she meant. It is hard to think of much good writing that doesn't reflect a deeply centred and located life, where the local and parochial have more value not less. And in any case, readers are not just sales figures, but are those whom writers have in their heads when they write, the imagined as well as the real. The conversation between writers and readers, the intimate spaces where exchanges take place and bridges are built, make what we call a literary life. Only then can a culture fully engage with other cultures from a position of strength.

Peter Conrad, in his mammoth 752-page survey *Modern Times, Modern Places: Life and Art in the Twentieth Century*, published in 1998, could only find two Australian writers worth mentioning. Just as they were at the start of this story, Randolph Stow and Patrick White are still there on the world stage – but no other author published in the last forty years from the other side of the world rates a mention. Conrad could be writing in 1964, the year he left Tasmania for Oxford with his trunkload of books. But it is too easy to read him as just the last in a long line of critics in another hemisphere who cannot see what is happening. I suspect he sees it very well.

The spectacle of the world's publishers with their samples and calculators going up and down the escalators at Frankfurt for a week each year won't be replaced by technology. But the publishing map is being reconfigured. Latin scholars, all fifteen million of them, have found each other on the internet. Which makes the immense effort required to sustain print runs of 4000 copies and often much less for works of literature and ideas in their country of origin look rather like running on the spot. As the boundaries shift between media and as electronic transmission brings the promise of other ways of delivering words around the world, only certain kinds of writing will 'travel'. The words themselves are already changing.

In 1945 an average twelve-year-old had 25,000 words in his or her vocabulary. Now, apparently, they get by with 10,000. My children read books, but other things are at least as important to them. They watch many more films than I ever did. They play music and paint pictures and design animations and websites and print fabrics and rock climb by their fingertips and work sometimes on Aboriginal cattle stations or meditate in mountain retreats where books are considered distractions from the soul's search for the real thing. And my youngest son has a highly intelligent best friend who proudly claims he has only read three books in his life: *Rumblefish*, *The Twits* and he can't remember the name of the third.

The books we once published are no longer in the separate section where I used to keep them but are now on shelves alongside all the others. They have always had a life of their own – their bindings, their typefaces, their changing imprints and colophons, the way their words encapsulate their times and, at their best, transcend them. I like to think of the ideas and imaginings and conversations they shared – on strange islands of the mind where meanings shifted and stories broke silences, where the play of fact and fiction began. And I know it's me the books have shaped – as only words can do. Other people's words are where I have lived.

Acknowledgements

To write an account such as this is to be reminded of how interwoven are our stories and histories. Publishing was once much more a group effort and McPhee Gribble's way of working perhaps more so than most. That work would not have happened without Diana Gribble, my friend and publishing partner for fifteen years, nor could this book. Diana has read it, corrected me about a wombat that was orphaned not injured and other facts where her memory is better than mine, and has allowed me to tell our story in my words. I hope that the McPhee Gribble chapters will be read as a tribute to all of our authors and everyone who worked with us during those years. Each of them was very much part of the story as I tell it here, but many could not be mentioned by name.

My publishing life lasted another five years after McPhee Gribble was acquired, first with Penguin then Pan Macmillan, during which time I was able to continue to work with many of our authors and with others I'd admired from afar. Diana joined Eric Beecher and others to start the Text Media Group and some fine books in recent years have come from their book publishing arm, Text Publishing.

Several people have been invaluable critics as I sought a way through the material to get to the bones of the story that mattered. Drusilla Modjeska, Carmen Callil and Don Watson have all contributed much more than they probably realize. We have shared ideas and perceptions, they have read drafts and sustained me when I found writing books much harder than publishing them. Jessica Little's suggestions were astute and will, I hope, help her generation understand what we were on about. Many others read segments or supplied me with information: Penelope Buckley who also went to Koonalda Cave; Clem Christesen who taught me much a long time ago and recently edited some of my colloquialisms; Jim Davidson, friend and sounding-board; Brian Stonier, who knew Allen Lane and was there almost at the beginning. The accounts of Australian publishing and of Penguin Books Australia could not have been written without the original work of Geoffrey Dutton. I refer often to his *A Rare Bird* (1996), as well as to Penguin UK's accounts: Steve Hare (ed.) *Penguin Portrait* (1995) and *Fifty Years* (1985). Hannah Lowery, archivist, University of Bristol Library, helped me access early catalogues and correspondence in the Allen Lane Archive. The McPhee Gribble Archive is housed at the Baillieu Library at the University of Melbourne and I thank the staff there, especially Jane Ellen, for their care and willingness to assist me.

My publishing colleagues around the world, and especially at Penguin and Random House, will, I am sure, find this a portrait of events they only dimly recall. The descriptions I give of words and actions are based on documents and correspondence in the McPhee Gribble archive. Robert Sessions at Penguin Australia was helpful. I thank Katia Zanutta, my assistant, always professional and an essential part of the process; Jacqueline Kent; Judith Lukin-Amundsen, who was there for some of the story, and at Pan Macmillan, Nikki Christer and James Fraser who have given me the kind of publishing support that is hard to find.

The book has been written with the assistance of a fellowship created by the Vice Chancellor of the University of Melbourne, to allow people like me time to reflect, research and to write, and I thank him and the University for their generosity. As I do my brothers, Peter, who read and encouraged, and John, who supported McPhee Gribble all those years ago when no one else would, the children who shared much of the story and especially my husband, Don, who saw me through.

The McPhee Gribble authors are quoted with permission as are extracts from the works of Shirley Hazzard, Christina Stead, Patrick White, Ruth Park, Miles Franklin, Donald Horne, A.D. Hope, Wandjuk Marika and John Wolseley. Some passages about Tim Winton and Brian Matthews had their origins in earlier articles: in *Tim Winton, a celebration*, National Library of Australia, 1999, and in my introduction to the reissue of Brian Matthews' *Louisa* by the University of Queensland Press, 1999.

Notes

FIRST WORDS

1 The account of the Faithfull Massacre is based on information
  in the Euroa museum and Roger Milliss, *Waterloo Creek*,
  McPhee Gribble, Melbourne, 1992, pp.245–53.
2 I am indebted to members of F. Truby King's family for
  some of this information and to two articles by Eric
  Olssen, *NZ Listener*, 12 and 19 May 1979.
3 My 'adult' perspective draws on an article, Julie T. Wells
  and Michael F. Christie, 'Namatjira and the Burden of
  Citizenship', *Historical Studies*, No. 114, April 2000, p.110.
4 Ruth Park, *The Harp in the South*, Horwitz, 2nd
  edition, Sydney, 1969, p.204.
5 Brian Coman, *Tooth and Nail, The Story of the Rabbit in
  Australia*, Text Publishing, Melbourne, 1999, p.103–4.
6 Thomas Hardy, *The Return of the Native*, Macmillan,
  London, 1957, p.79.

'A CREATIVE PHASE'

1 Later published in *Meanjin Quarterly*, Vol. 22, No. 2, 1963.

2   Two books have provided background and allowed me
    to test my memories of *Meanjin*: Jenny Lee, Phillip
    Mead and Gerald Murnane (eds), *The Temperament of
    Generations, Fifty Years of Writing in Meanjin*,
    Meanjin/Melbourne University Press, 1990; Lynn
    Strachan, *Just City and the Mirrors, Meanjin Quarterly and
    the Intellectual Front 1940–1965*, Oxford University
    Press, Melbourne, 1984.

3   Grahame Clark, *World Prehistory: an outline*, Cambridge,
    1961, pp.242–7.

4   A. Gallus, 'Archaeology of the Gallus Site, Koonalda
    Cave' *Australian Aboriginal Studies*, Melbourne, No. 26.

5   Ibid., pp.14–17.

6   John Mulvaney and Johan Kamminga, *Prehistory of
    Australia*, Allen & Unwin, Sydney, 1999, p.137. Some
    of the stone artefacts from Koonalda Cave have been
    dated as at least 30,000 years old and on stratigraphic
    grounds dates of 26–36,000 and possibly of 45,000 have
    been given by geomorphologist Jim Bowler.

7   Allen Lane to W.E. Williams, letter 25 October 1961,
    quoted in *Penguin Portrait, Allen Lane and the Penguin
    Editors 1935–1970*, edited by Steve Hare, Penguin
    Books, Harmondsworth, 1995, p.273.

8   W.E. Williams to Allen Lane, letter 14 July 1947, ibid.,
    p.47.

9   Roger Covell, *Australia's Music: Themes of a New Society*,
    Sun Books, Melbourne, 1967, p.205.

10 Wallace Kirsop, *Towards a History of the Australian Book-
    trade*, Wentworth Books, Sydney, 1969, pp. 11–12.

11 Quoted in Hazel Rowley, *Christina Stead, a biography*,
    William Heinemann Australia, Melbourne, 1993,
    p.351.

12 Quoted in David Marr (ed.), *Patrick White, Letters*,
    Random House Australia, Sydney, 1994, p.95.

13 Ibid., pp. 129–30. To the Moores.

14 *Penguin Portrait*, op.cit., p.283.

15 Geoffrey Dutton, *A Rare Bird*, Penguin Australia,
    Ringwood, 1996, p.52.
16 C.E.W. Bean, *The 'Dreadnought' of the Darling*, p.318,
    quoted in *The Dictionary of Australian Quotations*, ed.
    Stephen Murray-Smith, William Heinemann Australia,
    Melbourne, 1984.
17 *Australian*, 10 October 1964.
18 *A Rare Bird*, op.cit., p.69.
19 Donald Horne, *The Lucky Country*, Penguin Australia,
    Ringwood, 1964, p.239.
20 Ibid., pp.78–80.
21 Shirley Hazzard, *The Transit of Venus*, Viking Press, New
    York, 1982, p.37.
22 Geoffrey Dutton, *Snow on the Saltbush*, Viking,
    Ringwood, 1984, p.18.
23 *Patrick White, Letters*, op.cit., p.180.
24 Patrick White, *Riders in the Chariot*, Penguin Books,
    Harmondsworth, 1964, pp.215–16.

SOMETHING TO DO DURING THE DAY

1 *A Rare Bird*, op.cit., p.80.
2 Arthur Upfield, *The Widows of Broome*, Penguin Books,
   Harmondsworth, 1962, p.19.
3 *The Widows of Broome*, op.cit., p.7.
4 *Fifty Penguin Years*, published on the occasion of
   Penguin Books' Fiftieth Anniversary, 1985, p.108.
5 *Penguin Portrait*, op.cit., p.277.
6 Ibid., p.276.
7 John Michie, '"Community Standards" – it sounds
   alright – but what does it mean?', *Bulletin*,
   26 September 1970, pp.47–8.
8 Patricia Edgar and Hilary McPhee, *Media She*, William
   Heinemann Australia, Melbourne, 1974, cover copy.
9 Author's note, Gerald Murnane, *Tamarisk Row*, William
   Heinemann Australia, Melbourne, 1974, p.v.

10 A.D. Hope, 'Australia', in *The Penguin Book of Australian Verse*, ed. Harry Heseltine, 1972, p.190.
11 Jim Davidson, 'Notes on a Nationalist: Donald Horne's "The Next Australia"', *Meanjin Quarterly*, 1971, No.4, pp.444–5.

MAKING BOOKS

1 *A Rare Bird*, op.cit., p.127.
2 Ibid., p.121.
3 Helen Garner, *Monkey Grip*, McPhee Gribble, Melbourne, 1977, p.1.
4 Ibid., p.189.
5 Drusilla Modjeska, *Exiles at Home*, Angus & Robertson, Sydney, 1981, p.87: Esther Levy's 'Tribute to Vance and Nettie Palmer' was published in *Meanjin*, Vol. XVIII, No. 2, 1954.
6 Ellen Newton, *This Bed My Centre*, McPhee Gribble, Melbourne, 1979, p.19.
7 *Sydney Morning Herald*, 13 August 1979.
8 Arthur Phillips, 'The Cultural Cringe', *Meanjin*, Vol. IX, No. 4, 1950.
9 Helen Garner to Gribble and McPhee, 19 February 1979, McPhee Gribble Archive.
10 Helen Garner, *Honour & Other People's Children*, McPhee Gribble, Melbourne, 1980, p.52.
11 Helen Garner to McPhee, undated, McPhee Gribble Archive.
12 *A Rare Bird*, op.cit., p.186.

THE OTHER SIDE OF THE WORLD

1 Doug Lang, *Washington Post*, 2 May 1982, review of *Monkey Grip*.
2 Kathryn Kramer, *New York Times Book Review*, 1986, review of *Postcards from Surfers*.
3 Letter to Publishers 31 March 1989 and McPhee's

response 18 May 1989, Australia Council Archives.

4   *Bookseller*, 16 September 1988.

THE CENTRE OF THE UNIVERSE

1   Wandjuk Marika, *Life Story*, University of Queensland
     Press, 1995, p.140.

2   Elsie Roughsey, *An Aboriginal Mother Tells of the Old and
     the New*, McPhee Gribble, Melbourne, 1984, p.1.

3   Ibid., p.7.

4   Ibid., p.9.

5   Phillip Toyne and Daniel Vachon, *Growing Up the
     Country, The Pitjantjatjara Struggle for Their Land*,
     McPhee Gribble/Penguin, Melbourne, p.1.

6   Gary Presland, *The Land of the Kulin*, McPhee
     Gribble/Penguin, Melbourne, 1985, p.25.

7   Editorial discussions with Brian Matthews at first
     revolved around the kind of device that would set him
     free. First a series of fictionalized letters to A.G.
     Stephens was threatened, then, and more persistently
     through several drafts, a Female Diarist held forth and
     at some length.

8   Annear to McPhee, postcard 30 September 1987.

9   Tim Winton, *An Open Swimmer*, Allen & Unwin,
     Sydney, 1982, p.1.

10   Years later, Patrick Gallagher of Allen & Unwin told
     me they'd been kicking themselves ever since for
     their 'no short stories' policy, but was gracious
     enough to say that he thought McPhee Gribble had
     been the right place for Tim to move to at that point
     in his writing life.

11   Elizabeth Jolley to McPhee, 27 March 1986, McPhee
     Gribble Archive.

12   Carmel Bird, *Dear Writer*, McPhee Gribble/Penguin,
     Melbourne, 1988, p.123.

13   Don Anderson, the *National Times*, December 1984.

14 *Guardian*, 3 February 1989.
15 Helen Garner interview, *Australian Women's Weekly*, May 1985.
16 Helen Garner, *The Children's Bach*, McPhee Gribble, Melbourne, 1984, p.95.
17 Letter from Graham C. Greene to Gribble and McPhee, 8 November 1987.

A BREAK IN THE NARRATIVE

1   Rodney Hall, *Captivity Captive*, McPhee Gribble, Melbourne, 1988, p.48.
2   File note, 20 April 1988, Rodney Hall files.
3   Kaz Cooke, *The Modern Girl's Guide to Safe Sex*, McPhee Gribble, Melbourne, 1988, p.1.
4   Penguin later published Stephanie Alexander's hugely successful *The Cook's Companion*, Viking, Ringwood, 1996.
5   *Times Literary Supplement*, 14–20 October 1988.
6   Dorothy Hewett, *Wildcard*, McPhee Gribble/Penguin, Melbourne, 1990, p.3.
7   Drusilla Modjeska, *Poppy*, McPhee Gribble/Penguin, Melbourne, 1990, p.3.
8   Tim Winton, *Cloudstreet*, McPhee Gribble/Penguin, Melbourne, 1991, p.29.
9   Geoffrey Bardon, *Papunya Tula, Art of the Western Desert*, McPhee Gribble, Ringwood, 1991, pp.20–1.
10 Leigh Scott, 'The Early History of MUP' unpublished article, *c.*1961.

AFTERWORDS

1   Lecture later published as Miles Franklin, *Laughter, Not for a Cage*, Angus & Robertson, Sydney, 1956, p.3.

Index